SO YOU WANT TO PROPHESY!

PROPHECY MADE EASY

CHARLES ROSSON
INNER COURT PUBLISHING

SO YOU WANT TO PROPHESY!

ISBN 978-0-9797701-5-9

Published in the United States of America

Unless otherwise indicated, all Scripture quotations are taken from the King James Version of the New Scofield Bible. 1967 Printed by Oxford University Press and New International Version of the Thompson Chain Reference Bible published by The B.B. Kirkbride Bible Company, Inc. and the Zondervan Corporation. All New Testament definitions are taken from W.E. Vines Dictionary of New Testament Words.

DEDICATION

This book is dedicated to
My wife Priscilla Rosson.

ACKNOWLEDGEMENTS

I wish to recognize as many of the following as memory recalls and the untold multitude of believers who counseled me from my youth up. For, I am a composite of everyone who touched my life, by words, deeds and prayers.

First, I acknowledge my *Mother* who taught me what godliness was and prayed me and all of my siblings into the Kingdom.

Second, I thank my sister *Helen* (now in Heaven) who was a prophetess without knowing it. Her obedience to God and the Holy Spirit was phenomenal. Her display of a loving tender heart for God set me yet another example of godliness.

Third, I honor all of my pastors who patiently endured my ignorance and implanted in me the word of truth.

Fourth, I give tribute to all the faithful Ministers of the Gospel who preached the Word for me to grasp hold of.

Fifth, I recognize all of my instructors at *Lee College* who fought through my ignorance to lay the foundations of all of my study afterwards as I graduated into ministry.

Sixth, I credit my *Pastor Ceasar Brooks* who propelled me into prophetic teaching when my lack of knowledge was vast.

Seventh, I acknowledge *Sharon Stone* who taught me at *Rev. Bill Hammons School of Prophetic Ministry*. She went beyond teaching to prophesy into my life the vision for my destiny to train and raise up prophetic ministers in the local Body.

EPIGRAPH

Awaken to the Kairos

This day and even now the Word of the Lord is coming to me; and this is the understanding of what I have heard, "The days of waiting are over; now is the time to gather in the spoil of conquered enemies. Go back to the carcass of the lion slain in battle, look on the carcass of the fallen foe, and see how the bees have used the carcass as a hiding place for their treasures.

Reach forth your hands into the honeycomb and pull out the sweetness of treasures now yours. Make haste before others collect the treasures that belong to you. No longer wait for others to bring the gifts to you; they are distinctly reserved for you. No one else can adequately use or do the gifts I gave and reserved for you. As manna was only good for the day it was given, so also you must use the sweet, wonderful presents I have waiting your activation."

"The gifts that accompany your calling are both powerful exhibits of the calling and placing of you; but also verifications of my intentions and purposes of those with whom I have placed around about you. This core group is about to launch a bodacious plan that will disrupt the evil communications of witchcraft and false identities within the Church. It will happen so quickly the enemy will be stunned by the sudden attack and say what happened?

While he is so stunned, go quickly into his camp and completely destroy his icons and representations, lay bare his plans for full disclosure and exposure. Awaken the Church with loud trumpet blasts that call the Church to awaken to the *Kairos* time. They will hear the message clearly as a 911 emergency call and the response will be quick and devastating to the enemy. If some ask how can these things be?

I will show My power in manifesting the 9 empowerments of *1 Corinthian 12*. No longer will some sit back and ask, "Where are the manifestations of the Spirit?" They will be exhibited for all to see. You will demonstrate them in full public view. The videotapes of (Covenant Church) will be seen worldwide as the 9 gifts are openly recorded drawing even more to see and ask how can we do these same things.

The miracles of God's divine presence will draw thousands who will seek instruction and introduction to such power gifts. They will see with their own eyes and open hearts the indisputable proof of My presence and you will be there to reveal the "how to."

These are the days of your glory, no longer hidden in obscurity, no longer ignored as unimportant. So stand boldly and declare the truths you know and give demonstration of my gifts to empower the Church. You will not be left with unsubstantiated claims but visible results. The honey dripping from your hands will be licked by hungry souls who for so long sought such proofs.

Prophecy by Charles Rosson

TABLE OF CONTENTS

The writing of this book came at the behest of a prophetic word that was confirmed in my spirit by the Holy Spirit. That word given me several years ago was urged on me by my friends in the *North Dallas American Christian Writers* (Covenant Church Life Team), who made me a special project of prayer and support. The Holy Spirit gave me encouragement by placing in me a simple outline for the manuscript to follow.

Now, I begin my stumbling path to fulfill that assignment. What special qualifications do I have to undergo such a task? Believe me; I've asked myself that question many times. My answers are few and simple. First, I have been filled with the Holy Spirit since I was 15 years old. Second, I have been a passionate seeker of truth since that day of the Spirit's drawing.

Third, since my early 60's I have begun the pursuit of prophecy and its use in the local Church Body. Fourth, the years that I have spent in preaching and teaching has expanded as both of those fruits have matured. Fifth, the combined practice of the gift of prophecy with revealed knowledge of the Word has given me a better perspective on the ministry than those who have only a cursory knowledge of these truths.

The purpose of this book *So You Want to Prophesy* is to introduce every believing reader to a simple understanding of the spiritual gift of prophecy. In using *1 Corinthians 14:1* as textual starting point, note the emphasis of the text. "Follow after love and spiritual gifts but rather that ye may prophesy."

If, as some declare that prophecy is the act of preaching then there is a quandary. Do these proponents mean to say that preaching is to be sought after more than love? I think not. What is the proper rendering of this verse? I submit the Apostle Paul was saying "pursue love" because it is a lifelong objective not a one-shot achievement. And to pursue spiritual gifts but of those spiritual gifts prophecy was of the utmost value in the Church.

He then begins to set forth the parameters of *New Testament Prophecy* in the remainder of the chapter. I do not wish to minimize the importance of pursuing love nor of the other spiritual gifts. I wish simply to emphasize that love is a lifelong process of growth and maturity; this is a functional process that gives validity, acceptance, and power to the gifts.

This verse was never intended to negate the rest of the chapter and the gifts of the Spirit for next the verse states "...and desire spiritual gifts." The implication is that desire is a prerequisite for receiving the nine gifts listed in *1 Corinthians 12:8-10*. These nine marvelous manifestations are the supernatural endowments reserved for the believing Church to activate for spiritual service.

Besides, my purpose in this study is not to focus on the gifts as a whole but to give special attention to the passage "...rather that ye may prophesy." In this *1 Corinthian 14:39* the Apostle declares, "Therefore, brethren, covet to prophesy and forbid not to speak with tongues." Why would the Apostle Paul make this declaration? Because the entire chapter was designed to remedy ignorance concerning proper practice of the vocal gifts that is tongues, interpretation of tongues and *prophecy*.

Yet, even to this day much ignorance pervades the Body of Christ in this important matter. So this chapter 14 sets the protocol, purpose and the power of the vocal gifts. Once that remedy is properly applied, we can go further into fulfilling the injunction to covet earnestly the best gift, *prophecy*.

It is amazing that many studies of *I Corinthians 14* are badly interpreted by so many commentaries. The prejudices of the examiners have strained and tainted their judgment in making a clear and reasonable explanation of the text. Actually, the twelfth and thirteenth chapters should be seen with *I Corinthians 14* as a whole unit, not separate truths. They should not be seen as truths opposed to each other; often using a verse or two in one chapter to negate a verse in another. That is sheer lunacy.

The Holy Spirit is consistent with Himself. When read properly, the Apostle Paul does not put "other tongues" as unimportant or unproductive when observed with proper rules. They must either be exercised with interpretation in the public assembly or in private as prayer. They may be exercised without limit of time or use.

The Apostle alludes to speaking with tongues more than all the people in the Corinthian Church. If he did not do so in the Church, he must have done so in privately. The gifts were not intended to divide the Body of Christ into opposing camps of doctrine. They were meant to unite us, the Church, in power and victory.

So, with the prophetic direction to write this book, I began to see the plan and the purpose of the vision that drives me. I see a growing membership of believers who must be equipped to provide ministry to one another. As the human body has many systems that together provide immunity and the ability to fight disease, so also does the spiritual Body of Jesus Christ.

Those systems have the capacity to repel disease and provide curative powers for invading sickness. In like manner, the Holy Spirit has provided a redundancy of helps so no one is left alone to fight life's battles. Part of that immune system is *New Testament prophecy.*

This ministry *New Testament prophecy* is an antidote to spiritual burnout, discouragement that results in depression in all its forms, fear, and misdirection in life, frustration, ignorance of purpose, weakness, weariness, rejection, and disapproval. The list of negatives is endless and the prophetic gifting in the local church has answers to every one of them.

Imagine what the Church would be like if every one of us heard the voice of God clearly! What if every time I was subjected to undue pressure or dire circumstances that threatened my existence, someone would come with a *word fitly spoken?*

What if every time I was surrounded by clouds of confusion that kept me in indecision, someone would come with positive encouragement and direction? This is what *New Testament Prophecy* can do when properly taught and practiced. This is my dream, my vision to teach, train, and empower a grand army of ministry designed to be a healthy Body of Christ ministry. It is not my design to train people for the office of Prophet which is a prerogative of God to call them and place them. My calling is to train the Body of Christ in how to hear the voice of God for others through prophecy.

Do I have special skills to do this work? I have only the anointing and gifts supplied by the Holy Spirit? It will be up to you as readers and students to decide the worth of what I have deposited for you. Now, let's open the Word of God together concerning *New Testament prophecy*!

Charles Rosson

CHAPTER 1

SO YOU WANT TO PROPHESY?

*Follow the way of love and eagerly desire spiritual gifts,
especially the gift of prophecy.* —*1 Corinthians 14:1*

CB

Prophecy Notes:

☐ The Testimony of Jesus

☐ Prophetic Oasis or River

☐ The Winds of the Holy Spirit Are Blowing

☐ Speaking In Unknown Tongues

☐ The Purpose of Prophecy In the Local Church

☐ Putting a Face On Doctrine

So you want to prophesy? If so, you have taken the first step on a journey of blessing to others. Prophecy has as its primary purpose to edify, exhort, comfort and also to reveal knowledge and doctrine according to *1 Corinthian verse six*.[1] I encourage you to build the fires of that desire to bless to a white-hot heat; for they will result in attaining the gift.

The gifts of *wisdom* and *knowledge* must find expression in words for their meaning and purpose to be revealed to anyone other than the one who received them. I submit that *prophecy* is the greatest avenue to convey those messages to the Body of

Christ. The Greek word for prophet is *prophetia* that is one who speaks for God, a forth teller. In *Revelations* the response of the angel to the Apostle John was "For the testimony of Jesus is the Spirit of prophecy."[2]

The Testimony of Jesus

Thus every person who tells the testimony of Jesus is being impelled by the *Spirit of prophecy*. What is the testimony of Jesus? Is it a sealed book with the last chapter written, with nothing new to be added? If you mean the canon of the Scriptures, yes that's a settled, sealed book. But if you mean the testimony of Jesus today, no that is as alive as the promise of tomorrow.

The testimony of Jesus is living in every experience of every believer as they walk in fellowship with the Lord Jesus Christ. What is your experience with Jesus today? Does it ring with vibrant life and constant joy? Jesus is not a silent voice today! He affects the headlines of today and will be present in the freshest news tomorrow!

The Scriptures in the book of *Hebrews* declare that He ever lives to make intercession for us.[3] Yes, Jesus speaks today. Else, we would relegate the Bible to the dusty bin of mythological books of antiquity. To do so is to divest Christianity of all its life changing powers and to place it in the ranks of interesting but ineffective philosophies.

It is my assertion the continuing message of the prophetic to the Body of Christ is essential to the health and welfare of the Church today. It brings every member in the arena of participation rather than merely observers of an event. The fact the Bible clearly states we are to *covet to prophesy* takes us beyond the right to denigrate or deny and disparage the exercise of the prophetic gifting.

Have there been excesses of this gift? Absolutely! That fact emphasizes the need for proper instruction within the Church to equip and train the membership for effective ministry of that gifting. We have the manual for all the teaching necessary to provide effective checks and balances.

I believe God has heard the heart cry of the few and is responding by raising up the fivefold ministry to exhibit both by precept and example the benefits of the prophetic gifts. As the preaching and teaching of these truths go forth, the manifestation of the *gifts of the Spirit* will increase to the level the Father desires.

I expect the words of this book will assist in shining light on dark corners where ignorance once prevailed. So activation of the gift in the hearts of believers will begin. Knowledge without ACTION is wasted. God doesn't need reservoirs but rivers. Jesus pronounced that when a believer received the Holy Spirit that out of his belly would flow rivers of water.

Prophetic Oasis or River?

The problem with an *oasis* is that it is self-contained and only has one source of renewal, the wellspring from the ground. The *oasis* can never leave its environment to create new environments for others. The climate and geography in which it exists are desert and extreme heat. If that is descriptive of your spiritual condition, then you will need to go beyond the comfort zone of your present circumstances.

Number one, you may move nearer the solitude of the mountains where many rivers find their origin. Either that or number two, dig deeper the well that supplies your water. Or number three, find the artesian well that springs up without being dug. The *oasis* while it may be lifesaving to the desert traveler is limited in its outreach to others. It never goes to the needy; it stays permanently in its position.

An *oasis* is not the permanent dwelling place for most. It is the weigh station for sojourners on their way to cities and countries to dispense their goods. The confines of the *oasis* are controlled by the greatness of the water in its boundaries. How big is your well? Is its depth deep enough to support its ability to continue for many years?

However great the value of the *oasis* to weary travelers in the desert sands, the *oasis* does not compare with a river which has the ability to enrich nations. While the *oasis* surrounds itself with greenery and vegetation, a *river* brings the needed moisture for at least a hundred miles distant. The *river* changes the environment of all the shorelines it reaches. The *river* leaves its source to seek the ocean or sea that may be several thousand miles away. All the way to its destination the *river* brings fruitfulness and increase.

On its journey the *river* may connect with many streams and Rivers in their common objective. The environmental change is constant as the *river* supplies not only moisture directly to the land but to the atmosphere. Meanwhile, the sun draws in its ray moisture that fills the clouds which in turn is returned to the earth in the form of rain, completing its cycle.

Ask anyone who lives near a river how the atmosphere is made humid by its proximity. While the humidity may be uncomfortable during the hot summer months, yet the heavy concentration of dew and moisture are the perfect environment for producing great harvests.

Contrast that with the desert place where a mere canteen of water may be the difference between life and death. Yes we thank God for the momentary relief of an *oasis*. Our greatest praise is for the continually flowing *rivers* that bring year around, constant fruitfulness.

In *John 7:37-38* Jesus promised that we would become not an *oasis* but the source of *rivers* flowing. As we have noted, in the previous writings the Greek word for *flow* is *Rheo*. We derive the word *Rhema* (word) thus indicating the *rivers* out of our bellies would be words that are life-giving, life sustaining and life developing words.

When God would create He spoke words, in a practical demonstration for His children how to create or recreate their world. Among the first things that Adam, the lord of our newly created world, did was to name every living creature in the air, on the land and in the seas.

This was no mean feat for He named over 600,000 species of creatures and what he named then is what they were. What is your mouth declaring? Perhaps there is no doctrine being taught that brings more opposition than that our words have everlasting significance.

Satan's continual opposition to the prophetic ought to teach us something. Every one who attempts to obey God by speaking the mind and purpose of God have come under much spiritual attack.

Before false humility overcomes you with protests of your lack of ability or your lack of righteousness to do what Jesus did, let me ask you, who are you? Are you a child of God or an impostor? Have you been filled with the Holy Spirit? Or do you possess a cheap initiation?

Do you have *rivers*, or a mere trickle of small insignificant words? Remember the *rivers* inside you find their source in the Holy Spirit and demonstrate His character and power. You are destined to become *rivers* not an *oasis* that dwell under the hot burning desert sun. So open and clear away any rubbish that prevents the free flow of your *rivers*.

You contain within you the ability of unlimited blessing to those who hear with gladness the words you speak. Your obedience may contain the destiny of millions.

The Winds of the Holy Spirit Are Blowing

We are not to store up the manifestations of the Spirit but to release a constant flow of blessings to the Church. Church leaders take note; the winds of the Spirit are blowing. You can, as the sailor, learn to cooperate with the wind or oppose the direction of the Holy Spirit. To do so is to deprive the Church of power and destiny. A powerless Church is a travesty and an insult to the

Author and the *Finisher* of our faith.

Jesus has never been connected or associated with anything dead or dormant. He changed funeral grief to resurrection joys. So let those who lead the Church of Jesus Christ study carefully the Holy Spirit's instruction through chapters 12-14 of *First Corinthians* with open mind, as a whole not as separate treatise.[4]

They point to a continual flow of spiritual gifts bathed in *agape* love with emphasis on the protocol, the purpose, and the power of the vocal gifts. The emphasis is never a choice of either gifts or love but gifts filled with love.

When I subtitled this book *Prophecy Made Easy*, there are those who think this title ludicrous. If prophecy were easy then everybody would prophesy. To which I unequivocally state that every believer in Christ has, does and will prophesy.

They did so without realizing that they were prophesying. What then is the problem? Bluntly put ignorance! The Body of Christ as a whole doesn't know how to distinguish between God's thoughts or "just my thoughts". Also we have an exaggerated sense that only a "super religious person" could be used by God. (An attitude urged by many "super religious people.")

However, if God could only use perfect people then He would find no one qualified for service. So, recognizing our frailties the Holy Spirit comes to empower us for mutual service. Our lack of ability, knowledge, and power emphasizes the gift exercised had to be from God. How God loves to intrude into the finite with the infinite.

So let us encourage every trembling step made by a believer into the manifestations of grace. If they are laden with mistakes, give loving correction while continuing to support and encourage the effort. The *Corinthian* Church like some of our day was bombarded by the abundance of the apparently supernatural: soothsayers, diviners, witchcraft practitioners, false prophets and mediums, all of whom claimed their gift was God given.

Early Christians were at a loss as to how to distinguish the real from the false. It is in this light, the Apostle wrote these marvelous *1ˢᵗ Corinthian chapters 12-14* on the *pneumatica*: the spirituals, charismata: gifts, giving direction, purpose and direction for their exercise.[5]

Without explaining further the 9 gifts of the Spirit in the *First Corinthian chapter 12* or a lengthy debate on chapter 13, let us continue to chapter 14 which is most of our text for this study. 1ˢᵗ Corinthian 14, verse 1 says, "Follow after love, and desire spiritual gifts but rather that you may prophesy."[6] First we must "follow after love" and follow the God kind of love.

The term *follow* in the Greek means to pursue without hostility, to follow after, press, pursue. Paul later uses the word *Dioko* in his letter to the Philippians' church, "I press toward the mark for the prize of the high calling of God in Christ Jesus."[7] What was that high calling of Jesus? The *agape* love which was for him (Apostle Paul) and now for us is a lifelong pursuit.

So the attribute *love* we are to follow, but *spiritual gifts*, I must have a burning passionate desire for. That's an astounding statement to have a passion for the gifts. Why is this? This is the key to all spiritual gifting: to desire the gifts for ministry to the Body of the Lord Jesus Christ. The gifts are not divine play toys to enhance one's acceptance or position nor the finances of the one gifted.

These are Divine expressions of love to the needy ones in the Body of Christ. The third truth of the verse 1 *Corinthians 14:1* has been long neglected even by the Pentecostals, "...rather that you may prophesy." Prophecy is here delineated from all the gifts because except for tongues all the other gifts are expressed through prophecy.

Are you willing to seek passionately to prophesy? If so, then both you and the Church stand to profit from your search!

Speaking In Unknown Tongues

I must for the sake of clarity exegete *1ˢᵗ Corinthian 14, verse*

2 that deals with tongues *glossalalia.* The King James Version calls unknown tongues while not a translation was attempt by the translators to distinguish tongues spoken in the Spirit as being unknown to the speaker. This is correct. Verse 2 *"He that speaketh in an unknown tongue speaketh not unto men, but unto God; for no man understandeth him; however in the spirit he speaketh mysteries."*[8] So I conclude that speaking in tongues is speaking to God.

It is direct prayer that bypasses the senses because he speaks mysteries. Mysteries to whom you might ask? It's surely not a mystery to God. What could one possibly tell God that he doesn't know?

The Greek word for mysteries is *musterion.* It is outside the reach of natural apprehension and can be made known only by *divine revelation.* And is made known in a manner and a time appointed by God to those only who are illuminated by His Spirit.[9]

 To summarize: praying in the spirit gives me access to God praying mysteries to which my natural mind has no solutions. But the mysteries can and will be revealed by the Holy Spirit, in the time and manner in which I am able to receive them. The *Colossian* writer put it this way, "Let the Word of Christ dwell in you richly, in all wisdom teaching and admonishing one another, in psalms and hymns and spiritual songs, singing with grace in your heart to the Lord."[10]

Then in Jude verse 3 and verse 20 surround the warnings about false teachers who would urge the liberty of grace and forgiveness as the right to commit and practice lasciviousness with impunity. Jude verse 3 states, "Beloved, when I gave all diligence to write unto you of the common salvation, it was needful for me to write unto you that you should earnestly contend for the faith that was once delivered unto the saints."[11]

Jude verse 20 states, "But you beloved, build up yourselves on your most holy faith and pray in the Holy Spirit." Isn't it interesting that Jude does not urge honing your mental skills (although that would be good) nor does he suggest Bible study (although worthwhile)[12]

He does urge them to pray mysteries in the spirit which would result in them keeping themselves in the love of God looking for mercy. Jude verse 21 and verses 22-23 demonstrate how to win the straying ones; some with compassion others snatching them out of hell itself although their garments are spotted by the flesh.[13]

Praying in the Spirit builds up and energizes the believer. In the Spirit I am not just casting down strongholds I am building new strongholds of the Spirit. I build a fortress of spiritual truth from which faith hope and love can launch powerful attacks against Satan. Tongues are the entrance into the gifting of the Holy Spirit. Do not abandon tongues for they will constantly support you in days to come.

The Purpose of Prophesy in the Local Church

The writer of *Ephesians* instructs us with "And are built upon the foundation of the apostles and prophets, Jesus Christ himself being the chief cornerstone, In whom all the building fitly framed together growth unto a holy temple in the Lord: In whom you also are built together for a habitation of God through the Spirit."[14] The motivation, the direction and equipping the church is the fivefold ministry calling and commissioning.

A building begins with the foundation. A faulty or weak foundation will never support the building that follows and will never allow the purpose of the structure to be realized, therefore the warning of the Gospel not to build on the sand but on the rock. Our text declares that Jesus Christ is the Chief *Cornerstone*. The corner establishes the square, the strength, the true measurement of all the rest.

The rest of the building must fit perfectly with the cornerstone. Then the foundation of the Church is to be completed with the apostles and prophets (this already true of the Church eternal with the twelve apostles – where are the twelve New Testament prophets?) I submit there are many more than twelve apostles and twelve prophets that form the foundation of the many ages of the New Testament Church.

Look around at the Church world and at churches local many founded on breakaway doctrines from a schism in the Church. They were not founded on either apostolic or prophetic direction. I refer to a sermon I heard some years earlier from Dr. Cherry of Washington, D.C. The basis for his message was that many churches were breach birthed, that is, born butt first.

A method that is dangerous for the child and especially to the mother. Spiritually, the lesson is the head is the beauty and pride of the body. Most of the rest of the body is clothed, while the head is that by which we gain our identity, our knowledge and direction. While some churches are conducted by committee or proclaim that they are democratic, the Bible sets the paradigm for church government and that is theocratic and operates from the head down.

These patterns set for us the standard for church foundations and churches being birthed. The fivefold ministry must always act in congruency with the *Chief Cornerstone*. Jesus Christ is always our example not another man or woman. On the foundation now comes the superstructure with each board and stone fitly joined. In the original Temple every stone every piece of wood was precut so not a sound of a hammer was heard.

The New Testament Church is not to be beaten and hammered into place, but fitly framed by the Holy Spirit for us all to be properly located to beautify and strengthen the edifice. Each of us is involved in the administration of building up one another to find their place in the body. How grieved the Holy Spirit must be when the body turns against itself in self-destruction with harsh judgmental words that leave a bloody trail of victims for the birds of prey to ravage.

I have seen the wounds of those wounded in the house of God by those who thought they were doing the work of God by sending condemning judgment; their destruction was terrible and total. God can defend Himself from misguided error.

God has appointed none of us to sit in judgment just now, we are not capable of knowing all that needs to be done to execute those who err and sin. No, I did not make a mistake in my choice of words. I have personally seen the funeral bier full of those who were destroyed in their faith walk by extreme decrees of churches and church members.

Let God do the excommunicating if it needs to be done; does that mean we are to condone evil, sinful behavior? Absolutely not! But we do have the charge to restore those who fall; remembering that we also are subject to failing.

The purpose of New Testament prophecy is to build up the individual and collective believer. All too often the Church has looked like it is involved in a "demolition derby" with some ministries proud of the destruction that they have wrought on other churches.

No man has an anointing from God to do this! Jesus told Peter "Upon this rock I will build My Church." He has no interest in destroying the Church. If someone is doing wrong, show them how to do it right. Any wrongdoing will bring its own penalty without me becoming judge, jury and executioner. Christ is building the Church; let us join him.

Putting a Face on Doctrine

To teach you merely the doctrines of prophecy without showing you in practical terms how I arrived there would be both boring and unfruitful. So, I will tell you where I came from and my wandering steps to where I am now. I hope my errors will show you what not do. Perhaps enough of my successes will assist you in your quest to prophesy with excellence.

My journey began when as a 15-year old boy I was born-again and filled with the Holy Spirit. In an old line Pentecostal Church, I received my spiritual education. Much of which was good, however, some of which was misleading.

For instance we thought the gifts of the Spirit were exercised when the Holy Spirit "took over." I continued in that error of understanding through 18 years of pastoral ministry. I waited for the Holy Spirit to "take over" and it never happened.

This coupled with my fears of making a mistake kept me from prophesying or interpreting messages in tongues. Finally, I did something drastic; I quit seeking the advice of those who had never spoke in prophetic utterance to ask someone who did.

I asked the most profound question at my disposal, "How do you know whether you are hearing from God or when it is just you?" Expecting a learned and prolonged dissertation, I was stunned when he answered with a short "Charles, all the gifts operate by faith." Suddenly all my perplexity vanished. I had been going at the problem from the wrong perspective.

God wasn't the problem, my misconceptions were. Second, I was worried about my reputation, what if I made a mistake? At this point, God kindly interjected, "Charles you've made thousands of mistakes preaching and the Church has survived."

Third, I had made my biggest mistake by not obeying the Spirit. After I understood this at the next church service, I sensed the anointing of the Spirit to speak the words heard in my spirit. Thus began a whole new level of ministry to the Church.

Chapter Notes:

1. I Corinthians 14:6
2. Revelations 19:10
3. Hebrews 7:25
4. I Corinthians 12-14
5. Ibid.
6. I Corinthians 14:1
7. Philippians 3:14
8. I Corinthian 14:2

9. *Musterion* - Outside the reach of natural apprehension and can be made known only by *divine revelation*. And is made known in a manner and a time appointed by God to those only who are illuminated by His Spirit. *W.E.Vines Expository Dictionary of New Testament Words.*

10. Colossians 3:16

11. Jude 3

12. Jude 20

13. Jude 21-23

14. Ephesians 2:20-22.

CHAPTER 2

WHY PROPHESY?

I would like every one of you to speak in tongues, but I would rather have you prophesy. He who prophesies is greater than one who speaks in tongues, unless he interprets, so that the church may be edified.
—1 Corinthians 14:5

ॐ

Prophecy Notes:

☐ Why Prophesy?

☐ Why I Must Prophesy and You Too Must Prophesy

☐ Were the Gifts Passing Phenomena?

☐ The Purpose and Protocol of the Three Vocal Gifts

☐ The Blessings of Properly Used Gifts In the Local Church

☐ Putting a Face On Doctrine

There are those who oppose prophecy in the local church either because of lack of biblical knowledge or because they have seen abuses of that gift. However, the Bible itself supplies the perfect answer to the question why prophesy. *1 Corinthians 14:5* states, "I would that ye all spoke with tongues but rather that ye prophesied; for greater is he that prophesieth than he that speaks in tongues, except he interpret, that the Church may receive edifying."[1]

When the Apostle Paul uses the term "greater" he refers to

usefulness not station or position. Frankly, all the gifts of the Spirit are for usefulness not to enhance the one who exercises the gift. Is this gift of prophecy needed today? To answer that question, one need only to look at the Church in general today to note its lack of power, its negative approach to life and dependence on the world system to give a resounding, yes!

Let us look at *1st Corinthians verse 3* to see the purposes of prophecy in the local church: "But he that prophesieth, speaketh unto men to edification, and exhortation, and comfort."[2] Plus *1st Corinthians verse 6,* "Now, brethren, if I come unto you speaking with tongues, what shall I profit you, except I shall speak to you either by revelation, or by knowledge, or by prophesying, or by doctrine?"[3] Looking at these two Scriptures, we now have a fuller picture of the value of prophecy to the membership of the local church.

Seeing the purposes of the gift of prophecy now makes the question in the chapter title seem unnecessary. It is now an imperative for the health of the church, to have active the gift of prophecy! For all around us are weak, discouraged, ignorant and grieving ones who need to know of the Fathers intimate care and concern for them.

Why Prophesy?

Specifically, why prophesy? What happens when prophecy goes forth from a fellow believer to edify a weakened one? First, let's trace two Greek words that bring fuller meaning to e*dify* relating to New Testament prophecy. First under edify is *Oikodome* or *Oikos* meaning a home. Then there's *Dome* which is to build. Thus *edify* can mean to build a place to dwell.[4]

To build up a person is to give them a safe place of residence. It is also, in modern expression to charge up like a battery or to energize that which is run down. Second, *exhortation* in the Greek is *Parakaleo* one of the names and function of the Holy Spirit. *Para* is to the side and *Kaleo is* to call. *Exhort* means to urge one to pursue a course of conduct [always with the prospective of looking to the future.] [5]

There are times when all of us need to urge another to continue our focus on the future. Third, comfort from the word *Paramuthia* or *Para* meaning near and *Muthos* meaning speech. *Comfort* is a retrospective word having to do with a trial experienced. For example, a consoling word about our experiences that have become heavy baggage for us to carry.[6]

Generally, a prophetic message may contain teaching. Teaching about what, you might ask? It may contain explanations of hidden mysteries of the passage *1st Corinthians 14:2* containing the purposes and plans of God in our lives; how to achieve them and what has hindered their fulfillment.

The Divine teacher will recall to us forgotten dreams and rejected plans that God has for us. The prophetic message can even teach us our proper place in the Body of Christ. Prophetic words can reveal the secrets of the heart according to verse *1st Corinthians 25.*[6]

Secrets of the heart are often hidden to those who live in the soulish realm. I can be so sense conscious that I do not know how to listen to the Spirit. Thus the secret desires of my spirit man remain covered with doubt and denial.

The word secret in *1st Corinthians* verse 25 is *Kruptos* meaning secret hidden, akin to the English word *Crypt* which is a secret place. The revised version calls it a cellar. Things unspoken to any other person are taken out of the *Crypt* and brought into the light to be made known.[7]

Every descriptive word reveals the reasons one should seek passionately the *gift of prophecy.*

Prophecy Note: What Happens When Prophecy Is Unspoken

A prophecy unspoken is as baby aborted before it has a chance to live. So a prophecy must be spoken or written and read for it to take on life. Otherwise it becomes only a dream that has no purpose or chance of fulfillment. The world is full of dead dreams. The stench of death pervades the mind with hopelessness and defeat. Men then men sink to their lowest level.

The church as a whole has been filled with dead unspoken prophecies. These words would have lifted them from their rigid lifeless forms. The church without a prophet loses its direction and becomes stagnant, walking in circles in the wilderness awaiting the death of the unbelieving leadership. A pastor without a prophet will lose his dreams of excellence and sink into the quagmire of mediocrity.

The local church without the many voices of up building, comfort and hope, will miss a vital ingredient for health and growth. There are babies struggling with life's puzzles, there are battles with seen and unseen forces that seem overwhelming.

A prophetic voice is needed to give some encouraging words: words of new views on life, words of affirmation, reawakened dreams, and proper adjustments. These words would point the way toward success and would reinvigorate life.

Why I Must Prophesy and You Too Must Prophesy!

I must prophesy to those overwhelmed by weakness with words that build up then point them to possibilities of growth and how to get there. How many have given up on being able to become overcoming Christians? Better yet, how many would have gone on with *an encouraging word* (prophecy) at the right moment to propel them to victory.

I must prophesy because *a word of exhortation* (prophecy) would have challenged to greater effort one nearing the finish line of success. How many battles have you and I fought alone when just a word (of prophecy) that we were remembered and had the confidence of God would have lifted our spirits?

I must prophesy because there are times when the grief of rejection filled my eyes with tears of great sorrow. The grief of failed relationships has brought many to the brink of giving up on the worth of life itself. The grief of aloneness amid the Church has left many with emotional scars too hideous to look on.

I must prophesy for there are times when the Father has entrusted a *word of knowledge through prophecy* concerning events past, present, or future that would provide direction to assured success to the person I would prophesy it to.

I must prophesy because there are those who need revelation about false or perverted doctrines to which they have been exposed and correction is vital to their growth and development.

To keep silent when these needs cry for remedy is worse than neglect; it's a crime against my covenant family!

Were the Gifts Passing Phenomena?

I hope this study will provide more light than heat to any debate that may follow. Were the gifts passing *phenomena* of the apostolic era or a continuing ministry to be exercised today? Were they so confusing and divisive that they posed a danger to the Church of today?

If so, why were they given in the first place? Some have declared that they were needed in the infancy of the Church but now that we are mature, they are no longer needed. I seriously doubt the Church of today exhibits greater power and strength than the Church in book of Acts of the Apostles' day.

In the final analysis, all doctrine stands or falls on the Word of God, the Bible. The Bible itself is its best interpreter. Were the gifts promised for a limited time or were they for the Church in perpetuity? Many types and shadows indicate the permanence of the gifts.

In the prophecies of *Joel chapter 2:23-29*, we have been given the example of the former and latter rains as indicative of the outpouring of the Holy Spirit. The Apostle Peter cites the last two verses of this passage to explain the events of Acts 2:4.

The feast days of Israel are both protocol and prophetic of the growth of Israel and the modern day Church. Most churches accept the Passover feast but stop short of the feasts of Pentecost. In Leviticus 23:16, Pentecost was a new feast. It was a harvest feast. Pentecost signified the formation of the Body of Christ, the Church.

Pentecost was a first fruits feast. The power of Pentecost was exhibited in *Acts 2:4.* That day saw the reversal of the curse of Babel and the confusion of tongues. Now, with the birth of the Church new tongues were heard and prophecy ensued. The tongues of 16 ethnic varieties were heard coming from the lips of ignorant fisherman. So amazing is the uniting power of the Spirit when one message is declared.

The Purpose and Protocol of the Three Vocal Gifts

To more fully examine the pattern established in *1 Corinthians 14 verses 12-14,* let us focus closer on the protocol and purpose of the three vocal gifts. I chose these three gifts, because they were manifested more often than any others. Their prevalence is clearly seen in the overall chapter 14 in "everyone hath a tongue, everyone hath a song, everyone has a prophecy, and everyone has a revelation. Let all things be done for edification."[8]

Let it be established the problem was not in having the gifts but in the disorder with which they were exercised. Every gift had a function to benefit the whole church if used in proper order. As the result of their being exercised carelessly, they failed to achieve the intended purpose. As the result of their being used so often and prolifically, error crept in, bringing with it the need for instruction.

Why the special instruction for these vocal gifts? First, because the gift of tongues and interpretation of tongues have never been exercised in man's history. Second, even prophecy was the preview of a few men on whom the Holy Spirit moved in Old Testament times. Now in the New Testament, chapter 14:31, all may prophesy. Third, as the result, teaching was needed to maximize the value of the gifts.[9]

While some desire the order of the graveyard with all of its stone in perfect alignment, the order to be desired is the order that promotes life and growth. The greatest growth of a child is from its infancy until four or five years old. It is no wonder that some disorder was observed since ignorance abounded with no written rules until the Corinthian letter some 23 years after the day of Pentecost.

With no written procedure, everyone was left to his own understanding. To me, the greater wonder is why there was so little error in the Corinthian Church. Even so, many are ready to throw the baby out with the bathwater. Pastor, if your flock is ignorant of the use and the protocol of the gifts then it's your job to either educate them yourself or secure someone who can teach them in the use of the gifts.

Ignorance is always remedied by knowledge. The pastor has a mandate to feed the flock that is in his charge. The Word of God is the answer to prophetic and tongues problems. The greatest misuse is because they use the Old Testament as their pattern and not the New Testament.

The Blessings of the Gifts Proper Use in the Local Church

The spiritual eyes and ears of the prophet are in a constant mode of attention. For the only message he or she has a right to relate is the message they have received from the Lord. The computer of the prophet is in continual "download" and "print". Without the ability to disseminate, the prophet has no functionality.

Yet, it is at this point the prophet at the danger point. For, he is exposing not only the heart of God, the will of the spirit, but the deepest emotions and sensibilities of the human heart. This capacity makes him or her the object of satanic attack.

Satan will make every effort to still the voice of the prophets. For these voices proclaim and activate the forces of his destruction. For the voice of an Elijah can call down consuming fires on the altars of God. They will also cut off the heads of the prophets of Baal, and activate the rains of restoration to Israel.

The famine of ignorance that has been the heritage of the

past will only be turned around by the trumpet sounds of the prophets. This blowing of the prophetic voices will call to worship and to battle Jehovah's army. It is time for the Church of Jesus Christ to align itself to the various roles as God's mighty army.

We will focus further on *1 Corinthians chapter 14* to see not only the government of New Testament gifts but the blessing afforded by their proper use. In so doing, we will discover several truths that will alter the spiritual life of the local congregation for the better.

First, our attention is drawn to the fact of the primacy of prophecy in the local assembly which is attended by saint and sinner alike. A message in tongues, except where interpretation follows, leaves the entire congregation with no ability to receive understanding of what is being said.

Understanding tongues is by revelation in much the same way prophecy is received, in the inner hidden man of the heart. Unless, you think that is spooky, remember the entire Bible was received as the Holy Spirit breathed on men the breath of inspiration.

Verse 1 of this marvelous chapter makes an astounding statement to those who exclude the rest of chapter 14 as superfluous in view of LOVE. "Follow after love, desire spiritual gifts, but rather that you may prophesy." [10]

Why didn't the Apostle demand that we seek after love first, last and always? It's because love is a process that will meet us with challenges every- day. It is not a one-shot deal despite the old spiritual "Tis the old time religion" and its profession "Makes me love everybody."

That may have been our original emotion when we were born-again but soon our ability to love everybody was put to the test. We then begin to make religious excuses for our lack of love.

For instance, "I love them but I don't love their ways" grew popular. Most of which were "cop-outs" for us to act judicially toward those with whom we had personality conflicts. Love of the Agape kind is a process that demands we follow LOVE.

Putting a Face on Doctrine

It is perhaps here that I was especially prepared by the Holy Spirit to have a heart of mercy for others and almost always see the good side of people. Even so, being mercy oriented has brought me problems at times; for there are some people who only respond to confrontation. Being natured the way I am, confrontation is not the way I move.

As an aside, I will tell you of an experience I had teaching a class on the prophetic in Georgia. A young man who was chomping at the bit to exercise his gift as a correctional tool asked when God would release him to correct those in the Body of Christ who were living wrong. I responded "probably never" and proceeded to ask him how he would feel if I walked into his home and went to physically correct his young son.

Naturally, he didn't like that idea. So I told him neither did God want him beating on His Children. There are ways to confront people without denouncing them. A suggested life style change to reach the destination of Gods purpose will speak volumes to the hearer without intimidating or exposing the person to judgment by others.

God and I have an agreement that if I don't reveal negative things about others, He will not expose my frailties and weaknesses to others. Therefore I am committed to positive prophecy.

When I was in another state I prophesied to a young woman that all she wanted from her father was to be loved and accepted. Little did I know, as I found out later from her, that her father molested her under the guise that he would make a woman out of her. The prophetic gift enabled her to see that she was in no wise guilty of any wrongful doing and that she had acceptance with God her Father.

Chapter Notes:

1. I Corinthians 14:5.

2. I Corinthians 14:3.

3. I Corinthians 14:6.

4. *Oikodome* or *Oikos* meaning a home. Then there's *Dome* which is to build. W.E. Vines Expository Dictionary Of New Testament Words.

5. *Exhortation* in the Greek is *Parakaleo* one of the names and function of the Holy Spirit. *Para* is to the side and *Kaleo is* to call. W.E. Vines Expository Dictionary of New Testament Words.

6. I Corinthians 14:25.

7. Kruptos - secret hidden, akin to the English word or crypt - a secret place. W.E. Vines Expository Dictionary of New Testament Words.

8. I Corinthians 14.

9. I Corinthians 14:31.

10. I Corinthians 14.

CHAPTER 3

PROPHECY PERIMETERS IN THE LOCAL CHURCH

For you can all prophesy in turn so that everyone may be
instructed and encouraged. —*I Corinthians 14:31*

Cʒ

Prophecy Notes:

☐ The Pattern of Prophecy

☐ The Perimeters of Prophecy

☐ Defining Godly Edification

☐ The Path to Your Future

☐ The Holy Spirit Convicts

☐ Putting a Face on Doctrine

Each local church may have established regulations for prophecy in that local body. No prophet has a right to circumvent knowingly those rules. Some churches may not exercise prophecy at all. Again, I do not have the right to burst through those enclosures without permission from the Pastor or the leadership in authority.

The pastor exercises headship authority of his church. To exceed his permission is to enter rebellion which is the spirit of witchcraft. God will not authorize such behavior. So the first dictum would be to secure permission from leadership where you attend.

The second perimeter is to establish a record of character and reliability by attendance, circumspect life, financial responsibility (tithe and offerings), and giving service where ever possible. Then one can proceed to gain the favor of the leadership when they discover that you are not a flake or some off the wall intrusive person.

They should discover from your behavior, you are not there to change their doctrine or to impose ideas on how their church should be governed. Almost all negative receptions of prophecy are not for public revelation but for the prophet to intercede in prayer about.

The real question is do we trust our prayers to be effective? Public exposure almost always has a negative reaction and churches have been split and subsequently destroyed.

The 14th chapter of 1st Corinthians calls for prophecy to be judged for clarity, accuracy and content. Any prophet who is unwilling to submit to that spiritual law should not be allowed to prophesy. After all, the gifts of the Spirit work through human agency and are thus subject to flaw and error, unwitting or not.[1]

The biblical knowledge of the prophet comes into play. They may have a limited knowledge of Bible doctrines. They may have prejudices of culture and practice that can taint their prophetic message. So judge the prophecy not the prophet.

This is not a witch-hunt to pillory the prophet but an instructional time to improve the prophet's gift. And it's a time to preserve the Body of Christ from damage.

The Perimeters of Prophecy

In the seventies came the Prophetic Movement when God began exposing the fivefold ministry to the Church again. With the surge of prophetic ministries there is yet again the need for much teaching for the best way to demonstrate the gift to its fullest advantage. The Apostle Paul faced the Corinthian believers who had a deluge of spiritual gifts without a system in place to regulate order and to maximize the full potentials of the gifts.

Since the Apostle focused most of *1 Corinthians Chapter 14* to this manifestation of grace, let us do the same. The parameters of prophecy enclosed in verse 3 states, *"But he that prophesies speaks unto men to edification, and exhortation, and comfort."* [2]

At first glance, we think we have a full definition of those three words. But as we look more deeply into the Bible words of Greek origin we come to a fuller understanding of how the gift of prophecy is exercised.

Despite the disorders Paul saw, he did the proper thing by teaching and training as an Apostle (a messenger from God), laying the foundation for guiding weak ones toward serviceability.

I can make the argument that all the nine gifts are either activated or implemented through the vocal gifts. The *word of wisdom* expresses either prophecy or the interpretation of tongues and the same is true of a word of knowledge.

Faith initiates with confession and acting on the Word of God. The working of miracles usually begins with a proclamation of God's purpose. The *discerning of spirits* is revealed by words.

The *gifts of healing* are often first proclaimed in words that inspire faith: "Be healed" and so on. So, we can see that manifestations of the vocal gifts are needed to inaugurate the nine fold graces to uplift and bless the Body of Jesus Christ.

This reveals the value of the oral gifts and why they are still vital to the growth and well-being of the Church today. Our unbelief and timidity has left the Church bereft of so many benefits that belong to us and our children.

We now declare that it is a desire not only to know about the *gift of prophecy*; but we determine to activate this ministry in our own lives by learning to listen to the voice of our Shepherd.

Defining Godly Edification

The body of our study begins with the word *edification* by studying the New Testament examples with the various Greek words that define edification. As we covered earlier, the Greek word is *oikodomeo* which variously defines to mean: to build a house (in our case the building of life as a house for the Holy Spirit and our spirit).[3]

It also means to construct, confirm, edify, and embolden. With these definitions as a platform we will turn to the scriptural pattern of how to do the work building others up.

My first selection of scripture is found in *Acts 9:29-31*. I find this passage filled with humor when they describe a critical time of the church in controlling the over zealousness of the young Apostle in the making.

Speaking of Paul, "And he spoke boldly in the name of the Lord Jesus, and disputed against the Grecians but they went about to slay him. When the brethren knew, they brought him down to Caesarea and sent him forth to Tarsus.

Then the churches had rest throughout all of Judea, Galilee and Samaria, and were edified, walking in the fear of the Lord and in the comfort of the Holy Spirit were multiplied."

First, this new believer used his knowledge of the Old Testament and his newfound experience to dispute, and to investigate together but his reasoning made them so angry they sought to kill him. Seldom are men won by debate or argument.

My history teacher at *Lee College, Miss Nelson*, used to say, "A person convinced against his will is a person of the same opinion still." Argument and disputations usually end with anger, rigidity and refusal to admit defeat or wrong.

Most of us wouldn't give our opponent the satisfaction of our admitting, "I was wrong." When the brethren heard that Paul was on a hit list, they quickly ushered him out of town and sent him home to Tarsus.

The next word after his departure was when the churches

had rest. The comfort of the Spirit was not available as long as the zealot Paul was a source of stirring up difficulty.

Personally, I have seen those who destroyed every outreach of the Church because of their abrasive personalities. Few however, were the object of hit men. The same, more mature, Apostle would later warn believers not to engage in vain arguments and labeled jangling as nonproductive and injurious to the Kingdom of God.

Prophecy Note: The Path to Your Future

What are the paths of my future? How and by what means does God plan to fulfill my promise? When is God's due time to accomplish His words of my destiny? Each of those questions is valid only if I have made the decision to believe that God is alive, His Word is true and I have a vital relationship with Him. Having made the initial choices of faith, I can proceed to the other questions that most plague my attention and make constant demands on my faith.

Note that God has many problems in conveying truth to me. Much of my religious training may be good but there may have been an adulteration of imperfect knowledge.

My paradigms have been prejudiced by misinformation, misunderstanding and misconstruing of the words received. Yet in those circumstances I can extricate myself if I have a teachable heart and have built a foundation of enough solid truths to support my doctrinal integrity. If the principles that determine my faith are firmly established, they have anchored me to a position from which I will never retreat or equivocate.

Revelation begins in small increments before it can come on a grand scale. God reveals Himself more fully as I am able to receive and understand. The depth of the revelation is determined by the maturity and the ability to receive. God doesn't cast His pearls before swine.

So revelation is distributed along the pathway with small

deposits, never in total. We walk by faith not by sight. This deposit gives understanding of His word sprinkled with spiritual leadership. The Holy Spirit himself begins the process of my spiritual instruction.

All the avenues that lead to the wheres and hows have their origin in the imparted wisdom of God. As experience widens my relationship to the Father, His love expressed is the broad road to destiny.

The answer to how is in the unfolding wisdom of God which always has the answer and that wisdom is available to all. "If any man lack wisdom let him ask of God who gives to all men liberally..." His word known and acted on provides constant direction from a rock solid foundation.

The Word of God is designed to direct all of life's mysterious problems. The Holy Spirit is the heaven-sent minister to teach us all things. He administers understanding. He applies the anointing to equip and empower the believer to overcome in life and to give effective service.

The Holy Spirit Convicts Sinners Not Men

The Holy Spirit is assigned the task of convicting sinners, not men. We act as though men would never know they were sinners unless we pointed them out. Building the Body of Jesus Christ requires much labor but disorder and strife do not do the work of God. Strife is the tool of Satan to disrupt and destroy the works of God besides which most of our combat and contest is the result of personality conflicts.

I am not speaking of spiritual warfare which is never against people but against powers and principalities and spiritual wickedness in high places.[4] Identify your proper enemy if you would win the battle. The wrangling over doctrines, church practices of communion, baptisms, the return of Jesus Christ and eternal security are utter foolishness because none of them decide our salvation.

I do have my personal views on all these issues but I will not use them to divide the Body of Jesus Christ. Paul lived in the halls of constant debate over the minutest details, the Sanhedrin. No wonder he engaged in debate; it was what he was used to. He was a master of logic and reason.

Yet it was while he was banished to Tarsus that he received an abundance of revelation. I am convinced the desert time was spent in praying in the Spirit and building himself up on his most holy faith. It was in this time, he matured to full son-ship and where now he could enter his Apostleship.

Romans 15:2 says "Let everyone of us please his neighbor (which in the Greek means the one near us) for his good to edification." My responsibility is to minister the grace of God to all with whom I meet. Pleasing care will build up anyone.

Ephesians 4:11-12 says "And he gave some Apostles and some, prophets; and some, evangelists; and some, pastors and teachers; for the perfecting (maturing of the saints, for the work of the ministry, for the edifying of the Body of Christ. [6])

Unfortunately, this passage has been translated in many different fashions causing much confusion and disinformation given to the Body of Christ. In my more than thirty years as a full Gospel preacher, I was never given any information about the five-fold ministry. Consequently, I passed over *Ephesians 4:11-12* with a cursory glance never seeing either the purpose or the value of them.

Dr. C.I. Scofield exegetes these verses based on the word "some" meaning that some churches had apostles, some churches had prophets, some had evangelist, some had teachers and some had pastors. First, such an understanding fragments the churches into places where pride in their particular doctrines above the others separates fellowship with others

Second, can you imagine the chaos that would ensue if each local Church Body was denuded of four of the conduits of divine ministry intended for their up building? (I'm almost ready to abandon myself to this view when I see the chaotic condition of many churches because of their lack of the fivefold ministry. However, their lack is not because of the choosing of God rather because of their ignorance or inability to call properly into being those ministries.)

Have you seen a church without a shepherd? Who would recommend such a thing? We ought to have the same horrified response to being without any of the fivefold ministry! The Church would be malnourished, over balanced in areas and undersized in others.

Each of these ministries has parts to add to the building of a glorious Church. We have heard of the building blocks of good nutrition for the body. We understand the building blocks of a good education (whether in the arts or the specialized courses of medicine, etc.)

Yet, in the Church we have those who specialize in hobby horses of limited capacity to fulfill the mandate of Jesus Christ: "Go into the world and make disciples..."

The great commission meant more than get people saved, it meant prepare these new believers for the life that follows new birth. To get people born-again is not even half the job; preparing for life is a continuing process.

Putting a Face on Doctrine

Were it not for the fact that I know when I have heard the voice of God, it would be the height of arrogance to attempt to prophesy to anyone. However, the urgency of the message heard in the now about the future of someone's future constrains me to give them the message heard in my spirit.

I have nothing to gain personally by prophesying to another except the satisfaction of obedience to God and a clear conscience toward man. I may or may not be received. Has that ever happened to me? Resoundingly, yes!

There have been those who made my revelation, a joking matter. Others refused to receive the message either because it conflicted with their agenda or they had other priorities for their lives. Does that dissuade me? No my objective is to deliver the message not to force them to any action. My constant effort is to bless people not make people receive such help gladly.

All may prophesy and all do, most without knowing it. They may relate to a friend or prayer partner a feeling, a sense that God is moving in a certain direction, or urging them in someway. That is prophecy; it's just prophecy in an unthreatening manner. I am comfortable with my friend where I might be uncomfortable with mere acquaintances or strangers.

Chapter Notes:

1. I Corinthians 14.
2. I Corinthians 14:3.
3. *Oikodomeo* which is variously defined to mean: to build a house (in our case the building of life as a house for the Holy Spirit and our spirit. W.E. Vines Expository Dictionary of New Testament Words.
4. Ephesians 6
5. Romans 15:2; neighbor (which in the Greek means the one near us) W.E. Vines Expository Dictionary of New Testament Words.
6. Ephesians 4:11-12.
7. Ephesians 4.
8. Joel 2: 28-29.
9. Acts 2:4-11.

CHAPTER 4

REGULATING PROPHECY IN THE LOCAL CHURCH

What then shall we say, brothers? When you come together, everyone has a hymn, or a word of instruction, a revelation, a tongue or an interpretation. All of these must be done for the strengthening of the church. *—I Corinthians 14:26*

ॐ

Prophecy Notes:

☐   Who May Prophesy

☐   What May I Prophesy

☐   When May I Prophesy

☐   How May I Prophesy

☐   All May Prophesy

☐   Putting a Face On Doctrine

This aspect of prophecy needs clear revelation so no one should ever be ignorant of whom is capable and qualified to prophesy. So let us allow the Scriptures themselves to speak and identify the candidates for such ministry.

First recognize that we are not dealing with the *Office of the Prophet*, merely with prophecy in the local church. The *Office of the Prophet* is one of the fivefold ministries according to Ephesians 4. This is the choosing, calling and commissioning of

Jesus Himself.[1]

No one has the right to take an office by his own choosing. To do so is to take the prerogatives of God into human hands; the flesh is not equipped to do spiritual service.

Who May Prophesy?

With that said, who is qualified to prophesy? The prophet Joel proposes, *"And it shall come to pass afterward, that I will pour out my Spirit upon all flesh; and your sons and your daughters shall prophesy, your old men shall see visions; and also upon my servants and upon my handmaidens in those days shall I pour out my Spirit."* [2]

The very word came to pass on the day of *Pentecost* in Acts 2:4. What the early Church spoke as tongues unknown then were heard and known as prophecy to the different dialects of 16 different nationalities in verse 8. "And how hear we every man in our own tongue, wherein we were born?" and verse 11, "....we do hear them speak in our tongues, the wonderful works of God."[3]

Further in the Acts 10:44-46 in the house of Cornelius people not only spoke with tongues but also: "They heard them speak with tongues and magnify God." In Acts 19:6, "and when Paul laid his hands on them, the Holy Spirit came on them and they spoke in tongues and prophesied."[4]

And finally returning to 1 Corinthians 14:26, "How is it, then, brethren? When you come together, every one of you, hath a psalm, hath a doctrine, hath a tongue, hath a revelation, **prophecy**, hath an interpretation, let all be done to edifying."[5] Note the problem was not in the gifts but in the disorder of those practicing the gifts.

Paul did not urge suppression of the gifts but the orderly fashion of expression to maximize the gift. Then 1 Corinthians 14 verse 31 states, "For all may prophesy one by one that all my comforted." So here we have in clear language the evidence that all believers may prophesy. This was boldly declared and implied.[6]

Do not set impossible goals of perfection of either holiness or spiritual aptitude that would automatically disqualify you or everyone else. God only has people to work with. And through, just people, not angelic creatures that through some mysterious means have excelled far beyond "normal Christians". The truth is God is looking for normal people just like us to demonstrate super normal gifts to a much-damaged world.

God has designed the interaction of the Church to be the means of healing the many wounds the Church has suffered, some self-inflicted. Each of us supplies a support role to one another. Surely only God could conceive of such a marvelous plan in which every believer would contribute to the health and vitality of the other? What a concept.

Each of us carries a message of exhortation, edification, comfort, teaching and revelation that provides help and assistance to others. We have the seed to sow for a perfect harvest of 100 fold increase in every aspect of our lives and the lives of others.

What May I Prophesy?

Here lies the sticky point of prophecy. For it is here that most criticism of prophecy has focused. Many Pastors have had to repair the damage done by immature prophets or by those motivated by improper motives and bitter spirits.

Indeed it must be admitted that immature, untrained and unregulated prophets have done damage. They have tried to give directive prophecy that was destructive and intrusive. The obvious reason for most of this kind of prophecy is ignorance of the Scriptures dealing with New Testament prophecy.

Many of these misguided ones are not to be chastised too severely; for the fault is not entirely their own. The Church as a whole has not properly taught them, particularly the Pastors and teachers of the fivefold ministry. Ignorance is always remedied by knowledge and information. Arrogance and rebelliousness are character issues that demand correction before you allow them the freedom to practice their gift on your church members.

Most of these are young ones in the Lord and need to be treated with tenderness and patience. Recommend to them mentors to whom they will be responsible for approval. A harsh rebuke or a public rebuke may result in their never again trying to respond to the urgings of the Spirit.

To leave these fledgling believers or prophets to their own devices may be equally dangerous. Even in the Old Testament they had schools of the prophets where they could be taught and observed and corrected if need be. How can we in the New Testament age do any less?

The modern history of the *Charismatic* and *Pentecostal* Churches are replete with horror stories of the abuses of the prophetic ministry. However, there are also many times more stories of blessing and good that has come from properly executed prophetic gifts.

Everyone has to begin somewhere. Maturity is not instantly achieved. The Apostle Paul told Timothy to lay hands suddenly on no one. In other words, let them prove themselves and their gift to the leadership of the church, its Pastor and Elders. With a track record of accuracy, clarity and loving application of the gifting then that ministry can be launched without fear.

If we follow the path proscribed by *1 Corinthians 14: 3-9* and 25, the vistas of blessings flowing to the Church is an all encompassing opportunity to administer God's graces to the entire Church. When this pattern is followed precisely all areas of the church are benefited. Verse 3, "He that prophesies speaks edification and exhortation and comfort to men." [7]

If this trilogy was adhered to strictly no Pastor would object to prophecy in the membership of his church. This ministry would connect each believer to the other in mutual fellowship, growth and development. Each member would find his or her significant place in the Body of Christ and feel the connection of partnership in our Christian journey to excellence.

The Corinthian writer through verse 9 and 10 goes on to lay down a paved walkway for our feet to tread on. "For we are laborers together with God (what a team); you are God's cultivated field; You are God's building. According to the grace of God which was given to me, a wise master builder, I have laid a foundation and another buildeth thereon. But let every man take heed how he buildeth there upon it."[8]

What a magnificent statement with imagery that everyone can understand. "A field", "a building" both farmer and city dweller alike could visualize the metaphors used. In the building, Paul as the Apostle laid the foundation but others would help in the construction of the edifice.

You, who prophesy take heed, beware how you build on the foundation laid by a master builder. Don't do any shoddy work! God is a perfectionist in all that he does. He expects no less from us in the work that we do. Let us who prophesy do at least what the Hippocratic proposed that every doctors first principle is to do no harm.

Furthermore, verses 24 & 25 display a marvelous revelation of how God moves to make known His plans and purposes even to those who are hobbled by unbelief and misconception of truth. He makes it known by saying this, "But if all prophesy and their come in one that believeth not or one that is unlearned, he is convicted of all, he is judged of all. And the secrets of his heart made manifest and so falling down on his face he will worship God and report that God is with you of a truth."[9]

The word here for secret is different from that used in verse 2. The Greek word in verse 2 is *Musterion* but here is the word *Kruptos*, a secret, something hidden, akin to the English word *crypt* a secret place.[10] Just imagine it; the word of prophecy can drag secret thoughts and intentions of the heart out into open air for inspection and judgment (to ascertain the value, purpose of, and the weight of.)

The things hidden in the graveyard of the subconscious are

lain open to view, to bring healing, understanding of why we are motivated to actions that have long perplexed us. No wonder they fall on their faces in worship of God and so spread the news of the hidden abilities of prophecies.

When May I Prophesy?

Have you asked, "When may I prophesy?" The first place this was mentioned by the Apostle Paul was in the Church. *1 Corinthians 14: 23,* "If the whole church be come together ...."[11] The first thing to recognize is the Church in the early days of Christianity was far different in size and structure from most churches of our day. There were no mega churches or even large areas for meeting.

Most churches were home meetings. Note Paul's greetings to the church in their house and the early churches practice in the Acts to go from house to house breaking bread. The Apostle ministered in the marketplace where he practiced his craft of tent making then to the homes.

Also, he ministered in the synagogues and from there to the homes. The first churches were established in the homes of believers. These were of necessity for small group meetings where prophecy could more easily be accommodated. The large gatherings of modern day churches make it difficult, if not impossible to accommodate the congregation prophecy.

First, without audio equipment the whole congregation could not hear. Second, the leader of the meeting would have difficulty deciding who the prophet was before exposing the Church to the prophet whether a person of good standing or one to be avoided

Believe me; there are those no pastor would or should expose his church to. The early Church carried on a pattern they had learned from the Jewish Synagogue, where different Rabbi's would teach their interpretation of the Law often with conflicting testimonies.

Prophecy Note: God's Timing

I have seen prophecies given at inappropriate times, interrupting the sermon being delivered. Sometimes, a message would be contrary to the flow and spirit of the service. Were the prophets who acted in this manner bad prophets or false prophets? No, perhaps they were only uninformed, untaught ones.

Always the Spirit acts to benefit the Church or those in attendance. Many years ago in a church where I was pastor, there was a man who was a novice in the gifts who constantly interrupted the message to give prophetic utterances. There were two avenues open to me to correct this problem.

One alternative was to correct him openly and run the risk of destroying his confidence both in his gifting and the confidence of the congregation in his gifting. What I did was to go to him privately to give him both correction and encouragement. This was received and followed to the betterment of the Church and the fledgling prophet.

While on the other hand, I have given prophecies in the workplace, in my office, in my classroom, in the mall, for example. Everyplace there is human contact there is opportunity for prophecy; however do so with wisdom and restraint so as not to offend anyone.

Can you imagine such a church service today? It would bring conflict and confusion. God has designed the Church to speak with one voice. A true prophetic message will unite to truth never to confusion and division! Further enlightenment can be found in *1 Corinthian 14, verses 11-12*.[12] For who knows the things of a man except the spirit of man that is in him?

Even so the things of God know no man knows but the Spirit of God. Now we have received, not the spirit of the world, but the spirit who is of God. That we might KNOW the things that are freely given to us of God". So the inference is whenever and wherever the Spirit gives knowledge one should wait till a proper time within or after the service to communicate the message.

To this, I would add that communication should be recorded either in writing or on recording. This presents a twofold protection. It protects the person receiving the word (for reference and for presentation to trusted leadership for judging and remembrance.) The second aspect is for protection of the prophet from misunderstanding and misinterpretation of the message.

Prophetic messages have been received from every imaginable place. There is no apparent limit to where a prophecy may be given. Since God neither slumbers nor sleeps the timing of the prophecy may come at all hours and at anytime.

How May I Prophesy?

The Biblical patterns for prophecy are given in prodigious amounts in both the Old and New Testaments. However, much error has resulted from the inability to separate these widely divergent patterns. Most infant Christians and beginning young prophets are still attempting to prophesy according to Old Testament rules. They are not the same because they have different purposes and goals.

First, in the Old Testament they were dealing with spiritually dead people. (No one was born-again in the same sense that we believers are today.) So, God had to deal with them after the flesh not after the spirit. Hard-and-fast rules were established in the Laws of Moses to govern behavior and all outward behavior.

Nothing was done to include attitudes and the inner man. A man or woman was judged righteous on the observance of the legal requirements. If you kept the law you were righteous, if not then certain sacrifices and ceremonial cleansings could hold in abeyance the wrath of God's judgment.

Second, as the result of man's condition, God could only interact with them with conditions and varied times. We have the opportunity to live continually in His presence by the Spirit.

I am constantly amazed that New Testament believers look

to the Old Testament for proper behavior and conduct, as well as to try to establish proper patterns for New Testament prophecy. *Colossians 2:16* states "Let no man therefore judge you in food, in drink, or in respect to feast day, or in a new moon, or of a Sabbath day, which are shadows of things to come; but the Body is of Christ." [13]

Then in *Hebrews 8:5*, speaking of priests and patriarchs, "Who serve unto the example and shadow of heavenly things...." And *Hebrews 10:1*, "The law having a shadow of good things to come and not the very image of those things, can never with those sacrifices which they offered year by year continually make perfect."[14]

See also *1 Corinthians 10* and *11*, "Now these things happened unto them for ensamples and they are written for our admonition upon which the ends of the ages are come." The key word is *shadow* which in the Greek meant shade or shadow, darkness of error. Or another key word is *adumbration* meaning (to foreshadow vaguely; to give a sketchy representation or outline, to disclose partially) Webster's Ninth Collegiate Dictionary (1984).[15]

With this understanding we can see that it is not the intent of Old Testament writers to set standards for New Testament behavior in either personal walk or prophetic protocol. Otherwise, we would be duty bound to stone to death in public manner every one who missed the mark of righteous living or in prophetic utterance. Few would wish to live under such laws today.

As a matter of fact few would survive under such regulations. I cite just one scripture located in *Deuteronomy 13: 1- 3*, "If there arise among you a prophet, or a dreamer of dreams and giveth thee a sign or a wonder and the sign or the wonder come to pass, whereof he spoke unto thee saying, 'Let us go after other Gods, which thou hast not known, and let us serve them,' Thou shalt not hearken unto the words of that prophet, or that dreamer of dreams; for the Lord your God test you, to know whether ye love the Lord your God with all your heart and with all your soul." Even though the prophecy or dream is followed by signs and wonders and comes to pass, notice the proof of the prophecy or dream is in its message and what it leads to.[16]

Even in our day we are bombarded by new age prophets and psychics who are many times accurate in what they predict. Like the woman who followed the Apostle Paul and by her spirit of divination proclaim him and his followers of the highest God. While her prophecy was accurate and absolutely true it came from the wrong source.

It was demonically inspired to vex the Apostle. It was overt witchcraft designed to draw attention away from God to Satan's abilities. The result belies the miracle. Any miracle that draws me away from God can never be from God. Accuracy is not the true test of prophecy; neither is apparent anointing a test of God's approval of character or doctrine. God anoints His Word not necessarily my interpretation of it.

In *Deuteronomy 18: 20-22*, "But the prophet, who shall presume to speak a word in my name, which I have not commanded him to speak or who shall speak in the name of other gods, even that prophet shall die. And if thou shalt say in thine heart, how shall we know the word which the Lord hath not spoken? When the prophet speaketh in the name of the Lord, if anything followeth not, nor come to pass, that is the thing which the Lord hath not spoken, but the prophet hath spoken presumptuously, thou shalt not be afraid of him."[17]

To be presumptuous is an act of pride, insolence, shamelessness and irreverent daring. It is the haughty response of one who dares intrude on the prerogatives of God. Does this take place today? There are those who will declare "Thus saith the Lord..." when they are merely speaking from their soulish understanding and will. Some have even used the terms "Thus saith the Lord..." in fund-raising schemes both in local churches and on television telethons.

It is one thing to declare you believe something God has said but quite another to declare the Lord hath spoken. To declare, "the Lord said," takes the statement out of debate or contradiction and places it as a divine mandate! The prophet Balaam is a prime example of one who prostituted his gift for money. Yet, his are some of the most beautiful and accurate prophecies about the birth of Jesus in Bethlehem of Judea.

We are always amazed by the speaking donkey in that story; I don't know why? Asses have been talking since then and some of them are preachers. To get back to our theme, note that many of the prophecies of the Old Testament are still in the process of being fulfilled. So there was no way they could have been judged by those who heard them or read them. But the prophet could be judged by his character.

All May Prophesy!

In *Jeremiah 14: 14-15*, you can hear the cry of a true prophet of God being constantly assaulted by false prophets who declared blessing on a backslidden nation. While Jeremiah saw that without repentance, judgment would surely come. God told him that all those false prophets would die.[18]

God always remains faithful to His Word. Prophecy in the Old Testament was not primarily intended to minister but to proclaim God's purposes, plans and his will. (This gift corresponds to the New Testament gift of a word of wisdom.) This word is precise and brooks no explanation of man; it is God's determinate will.

 New Testament prophecy is prescribed in *1 Corinthians 14: 1-31* and is in the scope and range of every believer; *all may prophesy but not all are prophets.* Even in the Old Testament there were thousands of prophets but only a handful were named and are known to us today. Those who are placed in the fivefold ministry are those both called and commissioned to a ministry office.[19]

Those who prophesy in the local church body have a much more limited scope of ministry. Their message and practice are clearly described in the 14th Chapter of 1st Corinthians.

Simple local church ministry prophecy has as its aim and

purpose to assist in the growth and development of the spiritual, emotional and physical maturity of the local church.

Meanwhile, the office of a Prophet is coupled with the Apostle as foundations of the churches. As one preacher described it many churches were born breach birth (butt first) with out a spiritual head.

Normal birth is for the head to come first. For the head is the glory of the body and exemplifies all the body is to be. The office of the Prophet directs the Church. The Word of Wisdom and the Word of Knowledge are essential in his ministry.

I do not say the local membership cannot operate in the nine gifts of the Spirit; I simply state the fivefold ministry walk in or should walk in those gifts because those ministries demand it. It is a wonderful matter the Father does not leave us without divine equipment to perform the monumental task of winning the whole world to Jesus.

The motivation to prophesy and the supernatural unction that makes the gifts work properly is located in the Bible book *1st Corinthians Chapter 13*. It reveals a new kind of love, *agape* love. The *agape* love is a love not of performance but requires nothing. It is a love that is unearned. This kind of love is as supernatural as any of the nine gifts which reside in every believer's spirit.[20]

According to *Romans 5: 5*, "The love of God is shed abroad in our hearts by the Holy Spirit who is given into us." This potential source of God's manifested nature in seed form to be tended with care and husbanded with attention and care. (A peach tree requires 7 years to reach enough maturity to bear fruit.) So walking in the love walk may take years of growing in Christ to become fully revealed to others.[21]

The way to promote the growth of love is to begin confessing in your prayer chamber that you possess them. This promotes the identification with your new identity in Christ and not the old nature that was once yours. The 4th verse of *Romans 5* through the 8th verse became my mantra. I said it and included my name in the place of love. [22]

Charles suffers long...till faith arose to grasp these truths as a fact even when it was patently clear in my behavior that I did not act that way. I said these things in my times alone because others hearing me might have denied their existence in my life.

Especially in verse 8 where I quoted, "Charles never fails." For most people looking at me, I was not an advertisement for success in any field. When the gifts of the Spirit are operated in *agape love* they form an unbeatable force in both the spirit world and the natural world.

Love is the fertile field from which Hope and Faith grow to full manifestation. Without love, faith and hope could not exist; they owe their lives to love. Conversely where love abides it always brings hope and faith as companions. All the nine gifts of the Spirit are incredible manifestations of God's loving care for us. What greater manifestation of love could you demonstrate to another than to operate the gift they most urgently need?

The primacy of prophecy is evident from the resurgent interest and explosion of prophetic ministries in the last 15 years. The principal of this fact is that in every age when there is a new move of God about to take place; it is announced by a prophet or many prophets. The Prophet properly aligns the Church in worship mode or in battle array. In the individual prophecy the restoration of focus and the restoration of good health spiritually prepares the child of God for effective service.

Putting a Face on Doctrine

This is how I experienced this truth in my own life. Years ago, I was visiting my wife's family in North Carolina when news came that an aunt of theirs had died and that we should go to visit her family in another city at the funeral home.

Although not properly attired for such a visit, we went with the hope of rendering some comfort to the family. There I met the daughter of the deceased in a brief introduction. Retiring to a seat, I observed the usual occurrences at such an event. Most were ignoring the dead and had an inability to give comfort and consolation to the grieving.

My spirit within me began to hear these words, "Tell the daughter that her mother's days and nights of aloneness and bitterness are over. The difficulties of her with me were that she judged herself with a different yard stick than I did." The daughter looked at me in astonishment and asked did you know my mother?

I proceeded to tell her not really but I had met her once and had been told that she suffered from alcoholism. I saw before me a daughter who had suffered the anger and embarrassment of an often drunk mother who was unable to meet the needs of a growing child.

I saw a child who had to become her parent and hide the secrets of the family from neighbors and friends. She did so with great resentment and anger. Her mother was a Navy wife whose husband was often gone for months at a time, leaving his wife on a navy base where she had few to no friends. So she turned to alcohol for comfort or at least to deaden her sensibilities. It was with this information that her daughter could now look at her mother with understanding eyes and compassion.

The second event I relate is when in a prophecy class I was conducting, I was led to speak a prophetic word to a young woman I had never met. I told her the Father God saw her as a daughter of beauty and that He cherished her.

But then the message got specific in telling her that all she ever wanted from her father was to be loved, cherished and told of his admiration of her. I didn't know at that moment that her father had molested her in the guise of teaching her to become a woman. His actions led to her rejection by her mother who felt threatened by another woman, even her 8-year-old daughter. Notice that these revelations were not for exposure but to bring healing to secrets hidden in the graveyard of the subconscious.

Chapter Notes:

1. Ephesians 4
2. Joel ; Acts 2:4
3. Acts 2:8,11
4. Acts 10:44-46; Acts 19:6
5. 1 Corinthians 14:26
6. 1 Corinthians 14:31
7. 1 Corinthians 14:3-9; 25.
8. 1 Corinthians 14:9,10.
9. 1 Corinthians 14:24,25.
10. *Kruptos*, a secret; something hidden, akin to the English word *Crypt* a secret place. W.E. Vines Expository Dictionary of New Testament Words.
11. 1 Corinthians 14: 23.
12. 1 Corinthians 14:11,12.
13. Colossians 2:16
14. Hebrews 8:5; 10:1
15. 1 Corinthians 10, 11
16. Deuteronomy 13:1-3
17. Deuteronomy 18:20-22
18. Jeremiah 14:14-15
19. 1 Corinthians 14: 1-13
20. *Agape love* is a love not of performance but requires nothing. It is a love that is unearned. W.E. Vines Expository Dictionary of New Testament Words.
21. Romans 5:5
22. Romans 5:8

CHAPTER 5

PROPHECY AND THE GIFTS OF THE HOLY SPIRIT

But everyone who prophesies speaks to men for their
strengthening, encouragement and comfort. —*I Corinthians 14:3*

☙

Prophecy Notes:

- ☐ Covet to Prophesy
- ☐ The Gifts of the Holy Spirit & Prophecy
- ☐ Prophetic Invitation
- ☐ Prophesy Within the Limits of Your Influence
- ☐ Knowing the Span of Your Reach
- ☐ Putting a Face on Doctrine

We are told to desire "spiritual gifts" but I wonder if those who oppose gifts do so. The word desire is *Zeloo* which means to have a zeal for, to seek or desire earnestly the object of warm interest.[1] It is the picture of passionate interest that will not rest until the object of that attention is realized. Are you passionately seeking for some means to bless the Body of Jesus Christ?

Third, of all things Paul said seek to prophesy above all. Again, let us attempt to answer the question "Why prophesy?" When one inspects the list of the nine gifts of the Spirit, we see so many great charismas each of which we can see have tremendous value in the Body.

I remember well when healing ministries were birthed in the late forties and early fifties by *Oral Roberts, A. A. Allen, Jack Coe* and a myriad of other men who had huge tents with ten thousand seat capacities that were filled nightly with earnest seekers.

The Church became full of men and women who sought the *gifts of healing*. Then the charismatic renewal came when mainline Protestants and Catholics began to be filled with the Holy Spirit. With this movement came again the need for instruction in how to manifest the *gift of tongues* properly.

Covet to Prophesy

The purpose of this chapter is not to give a detailed explanation of each of the nine gifts of the Spirit. Rather, it is to offer an overview of their relationship to prophecy. In so doing, we will see why we are enjoined by verse 3 of *Corinthians 14* to covet to prophesy. Since the first gift manifested on the day of Pentecost by believers was *tongues* and tongues are to speak to God according to verse 2. There must be a reason for that gift being used first. I wish to point out several reasons for us to explore.[2]

Reason number one being *tongues* brings us into instant communication with the Father God. And communication is the heart of communion and fellowship. Dialogue is conversation between two people. I talk to God and God talks to me.

Reason number two is, I don't always know what to pray for as I ought.[3] So, divine assistance is given by the Holy Spirit in groans that cannot be spoken in *articulate speech* according to the will of the Father.

Reason three reveals the one who speaks in *tongues* edifies himself. This is no small matter for each one of us has the need for building ourselves up on occasion. It is always better to minister from the strength of restored resources of the Spirit than form a depleted spirit.

Reason number four is *tongues* are an expeditor and initiator of the gifts. I refer to the many times when people in the Book of Acts spoke with tongues they are then said to have prophesied.[4]

The Gifts of the Holy Spirit and Prophecy

Note the *word of wisdom* can only be revealed by prophecy; speaking for God. The *word of wisdom* is the revelation of God's determinate will. This is a "Thus saith the Lord..." In this revelation, there are no ifs, ands or maybes. This is exactly what God is going to do.

You may notice that in the following order wisdom precedes knowledge. This is a reversal of the natural order that wisdom is the ability to apply knowledge wisely. So, God's idea of wisdom and ours are at variance. Our normal application of what wisdom is out of order and therefore incorrect. The *word of wisdom* is far deeper than that. I am convinced the Old Testament prophecies were in fact the *word of wisdom* speaking God's predetermined WILL.

Then we look into the *word of knowledge* the ability supernaturally given to KNOW acts, words and events beyond the reach of our natural apprehension. This is not information received as the result of a witch-hunt or spurious gossip. It is just knowing you know some fact or event and having no reasonable explanation other than you know.

But that revelation cannot be conveyed without the *gift of prophecy*. That is one reason people are fearful of the prophet; they are afraid that he is a mind reader, ready to expose every secret sin. The only things the prophet sees are the things that God reveals and plans for restoration and healing.

Even the gift of FAITH is always expressed with words, hence *prophecy*. Words of declaration: "Rise and be healed." Words of affirmation "I see you rising from the pit in which you have been wallowing in self-denial and mistrust." That special endowment is most often expressed in words.

The *gifts of healing* are preceded by WORDS to challenge to believe and to receive which are again PROPHETIC. The one who exercises the gift is always giving WORDS of encouragement and WORDS of his declared belief of what God is going to do. In other words, he prophesies.

The *workings of miracles are* involved with forth telling if not foretelling, either before the event, during the event or after the event. Many people would not be able to recognize the miracle if it were not the miracle were identified as to its source by prophetic proclamation.

The *discerning of spirits* is often the most misnamed gift of the Spirit. This is a highly specific ministry. It is not discerning events or intents. It is the *discerning of spirits*. This may include the naming of the spirit being manifested but is most certainly identifying either by spiritually sensing or seeing through the eyes of the spirit the spiritual entity.

Through this gifting I may see angels or demonic presences or I may only sense those presences. There is a knowing of the attitudes and motivations at their source. But that gift is expressed by prophetic speech. Again this is forth telling, not necessarily foretelling.

The *various kinds of tongues* include both the languages of men and of angels. I may speak in languages unknown to me but known to others in the assembly. However, if I were to speak the language of angels I then am addressing a different audience for a different purpose. Since angels are messengers of God, we may be exchanging Gods coded messages for spiritual battle strategies. But in either case prophecy is involved.

The interpretation of tongues becomes the equivalent of *prophecy* with a specific purpose: the telling forth what the unknown tongue has been speaking. It is not a translation but an interpretation. It gives the meaning of what has been spoken.

When the interpretation is spoken it becomes *prophecy*. I often say the two gifts are triggered by different things. Interpretation of tongues is a response to the actions of another. *Prophecy* is a response to the inner working of the Holy Spirit. It is a response to God not necessarily a response to someone else. Through this review, we see the interrelationship of the nine gifts. There is a harmonious working with no place for jealousy or the spirit of competition.

The Prophetic Invitation

With the hearing ear, I hear, and with the seeing eye I see. The mysteries of the Father in sight and sound unfold with the panorama of vision and a symphony of melodious power. I invite you into a level of understanding and receptivity beyond what you now experience.

Many in the Church world are still ignorant of their purpose and destiny. While they admire those they believe to be heroes and heroines of the faith, they continue to wallow in mediocrity as those who have no position, nor plan for the future. They remain unproductive in the Kingdom and even worse are the cause of blockage, a veritable dam to the flow of God's blessings to our generation.

The hearing ear hears the cries of troubled ones who are desperate to reach new levels of faith and accomplishment in their lives. Without the hearing ear, their cries go unanswered. Instead of possessing a hearing ear, they are surrounded by the myriad of voices screeching insults and accusations, indictments of real or imagined failures. They wallow in the quagmire of sins already forgiven and forgotten by the Father. Yet their guilt persists.

With the hearing ear they would know the freedom given to every believer in *Romans 8*. Sadly, without the hearing ear, they have a nightmare focused on past errors. Hopelessness pervades their horizons. But wait! There is another voice to be heard. I hear a voice of hope, joy and the prophecies of dreams I always wanted and aspired to.[4]

This change of direction for me came when I finally made a decision to hear the voice of God. I would listen from the premise of faith and not of doubt and fear. My confession became "I hear the voice of God for He is in constant communication with my spirit." Was it as simple as that? No I stumbled with trial and error, just as anyone else. I learned from two sources how to discern the true voice of the Father. First and foremost, The Word of God, the Bible, is my source for hearing God.

Is what I hear supported by the intent of the Word of God? Is it consistent with the nature and character of God? With this as a basis I can make a proper evaluation and estimation of the voice I hear. Second, the relationship I have with the Father determines the depth of the secrets He will share with me.

The calling and opportunity that I have to share the message will also be a determining factor in what kind of message He will share with me. (For instance he will not flood me with world-shaking prophecies when I have no platform to deliver them to the world.)

Nor will he give me Church affecting prophecies without giving a voice to be heard by leadership. Many are looking for a worldwide ministry so they will become overnight sensations, rather than affecting the world in which they live and have influence. The personal knowledge I have of Jesus Christ and His character will establish the ear with which I hear.

The "seeing eye" looks into the revealed plans of God for the future. The brightest hopes of splendor reveal themselves to the "seeing eye". It is amazing how many walk with directionless steps and stumble across the favor of God accidentally. The "seeing eye" walks with confident steps into tomorrow because they have seen tomorrow today. This is not a blind leap of faith, actually there is no such thing as blind faith!

All of faith is based on thus "saith the Lord," or "I know whom I have believed and am persuaded that He is able keep (or retain) that which I have committed unto Him against that day." The outlook of the "seeing eye" is always upward. Isaiah saw the Lord high and lifted up and was propelled into the life of a prophet. No one ever prophecies wisely or correctly who only sees and smells the brimstone of judgment and doom.

Isaiah saw and smelled the smoke of God's presence, the *Shekinah Glory,* whose train filled the temple (What do you see when you look in your temple that is your spirit?) This was not the smoke of judgment but presence of power and blessing. His presence announces the favor of promised destiny. Isaiah left behind his awe of King Uzziah to see the awesomeness of God.[5]

Prophesy Within the Limits of Your Influence

In looking at the initial chapters of each of the prophets of the Old Testament, you will find that they were given definite areas and definite groups of people to prophesy to. In other words their prophecies were given specific areas of influence.

Isaiah was to prophesy to Judah and Jerusalem during the days of Ussiah, Jotham and Hezekiah the kings of Judah. This was his original sphere of influence. However in those directed words there was a ripple effect that reaches even to us today and beyond. Such is the power of prophecy to reach beyond today to affect and effect generations not yet living.

But specifically Isaiah prophesied to a designated people and time. He did not know the extent to which his prophesies would reach. Jeremiah comes along later with further prophesies to Judah in the reigns of Kings Josiah, Jehoiakim, and Zedekiah.

Ezekiel prophesied to the nation of Israel. Daniel prophesied to exiled and captive Judah. On and on, we could go to identify the spheres of prophetic influence of each of these wonderful men of God but it is not needed to further establish our point. Each of these men had a specific calling and place to serve for their unique ministries.

That they leaped through generations and though long dead they yet speak today is only proof the Word of God is timeless. Anointed words have eternity in their DNA. Jesus said of his own words in John 6:63.....The words that I speak unto you, "They are spirit and they are life." The obedience of men to prophesy bears eternal consequences![6]

Think of it; you may contain the key to someone's future. You may have the words that uplift a falling one. You may change the destiny of a generation that is now being formed.

Prophecy Note: When Did I Know?

My personal experiences are both an explanation of how I knew that I had entered the office of a Prophet and what was the sphere of my influence. On entering the office of the Prophet, I began to notice that my prophecies took on a larger context.

So much so, the pastor appointed me the Prophet of the church. (Please note; you are not a prophet to anyone, unless they accept you as such.) Prophecies that were once more individualized now were expanded in scope for the church I attended and its place in our community.

I received prophecies that declare direction of where the church was headed and what its destiny could be. The pastor later declared the prophecies were given before every move of God in our midst. I say this not in pride but to illustrate the point in reference: prophesy within the limits of your influence.

To further illustrate the lesson, I went from Augusta, Georgia to visit my daughter in Dallas Texas. I knew that during my time there she was hoping that I would have a prophetic word for her. That whole time I sought to hear from God a message specifically for her, nothing came.

Afterwards, as I came into the airspace around Atlanta, Georgia the prophetic reception was turned, the air came alive to me with prophetic revelation. The basic understanding I received was this: My sphere of prophetic ministry was Augusta not Dallas. Don't over learn the lesson.

God was teaching me a lesson on my sphere of influence. This was not to forbid me to prophesy anywhere but my local church in Augusta.

No you may prophesy anywhere at anytime the Spirit so directs. Recognize that your primary place of prophecy is where you have the most influence.

Second if no revelation comes, don't come under constraint and manufacture a word of prophecy. If someone asks for a word and nothing comes forth at that moment, tell them you will pray about the matter and get with them later, if Gods supplies a word.

Knowing The Span of Your Reach

What is the span of your reach? That depends on what reach we're discussing. If we were discussing physical reach? That is determined by my physical DNA. Did I mean intellectual? That again has its basis in my DNA but also my desire to learn and the amount of effort I am willing to expend in the pursuit of knowledge. Spiritually, I have unlimited boundaries within the span of my reach.

In an obscure countryside that surrounded a small sea, The Sea of Galilee, were a few men who would form the nucleus of those twelve men who formed the foundation of the New Testament Church. They sit in an everlasting position because the Church of Jesus Christ is everlasting. These men far exceeded their span of reach in every area of their lives. They traveled to all the corners of their known world. Even today their names and writings are known and honored after two thousand years have passed.

You, in whatever station, you started in are empowered to impact generations in the future. Your physical limitations, intellectual prowess, emotional strength, cultural background or social status in no way set the boundaries for world affecting, world changing impact.

You can reach beyond your span of reach through the Holy Spirit. Within you is a vast reservoir of untapped resources. There are rivers of blessing waiting to flow forth in <u>bank overflowing blessings</u> to the entire world. Yours are the resources that will make glad the nations!

Rivers of blessings that bring restoration to depleted ones, rivers that bring love's assistance to those dying of thirst for the cool waters of love. I am not speaking of a cup full or of buckets of grace but rivers flowing out from your belly. The bubbling spring within you will supply rivers of mercy and grace to a sin darkened world.

Even in those times when you feel dry emotionally, physically drained and spiritually burned-out, you have more life sustaining moisture than some have ever experienced. Besides, you know how to refresh yourself. You learned the secret place of renewal years ago.

So return to the oasis of private devotions to bathe again in the cleansing restorative powers of fellowship with the Father. You know how to do this. Again, I say you learned how to years ago. This has been the secret of your passion and power. Activate it daily for you are on a journey to destiny.

Putting a Face On Doctrine

I will not relate a personal experience with every gift recorded in the Scriptures. There are several reasons for this, the main one because I am not proficient in all the gifts. Another one is I have had limited experience in several of the gifts. So I will briefly mention some experiences that I believe worthwhile.

On one occasion, I received the *word of knowledge* that a person whom the Spirit revealed to me was stealing money out of the offering basket of the church as it passed by. I was immediately faced with a dilemma. What or how much did I dare reveal. I quickly realized that I dare not reveal any of that information to the church.

That would have precluded any restoration and healing for the person involved and meant probable immediate anger and excommunication of the offending person. The revelation was not for exposure but for healing, intercession and correction. All of which could be done without confrontation and exposure.

The *gift of the interpretation of tongues* was my first introduction to the prophetic ministry. This was my launching pad for other gifts that would follow. After I began my timorous steps into the uncertainties of utterance that required all the faith I could muster, there eventually came confidence till it was no longer a question but a certainty that I was delivering the message of God at that moment.

The *discernment of spirits* came on at least three occasions in my early ministry. One of which I remember vividly. I had just returned home from an evangelistic effort. My dad brought home a friend from work to share some pictures that my older brother had done in pastel chalk.

After proudly showing the accomplishments of his son and introducing me as his preacher son, the man whom dad had introduced spoke complimentary words to both my father and to me.

After he left, without much thought I said to my Dad "Do you know what is wrong with that man?" To which my father replied, "No, I don't; no one seems to like him for no apparent reason. What is wrong with him?"

I cannot tell you why I responded as I did but quickly I replied, "He is demon possessed." My mother later told me that I had shaken my dad up. For the man I had met that night was a dealer in pornography when all that material was illegal.

I have pronounced healing and I have announced the knowing the gift of faith brings. Is it any wonder why I consider so highly the *gift of prophecy*?

Chapter Notes:

1. Zeloo which means to have zeal for; to seek or desire earnestly the object of warm interest. *W.E.Vines Expository Dictionary of New Testament Words.*

2. I Corinthians 14:2, 3.
3. Romans 8:26.
4. Book of Acts.
5. Romans 8.
6. Exodus 34:6,7.
7. John 6:63.

CHAPTER 6

TRAINING YOUR SPIRIT WITH THE WORD OF GOD

In fact, though by this time you ought to be teachers, you need someone to teach you the elementary truths of God's word all over again. You need milk not solid food. —Hebrews 5:12

ॐ

Prophecy Notes:

- ☐ The Power of Plain Words
- ☐ Understanding the Word of Righteousness
- ☐ Aligning Our Minds with the Foundation of Truth
- ☐ 12 Steps to Training Your Spirit to Discern Good & Evil
- ☐ The Result of Training Your Spirit with the Word of God
- ☐ Putting a Face on Doctrine

The writer of the great letter to the Hebrew Jews scattered throughout the world, addresses why He cannot now explain deeper mysteries of the Word to them. They are not able to digest and understand them yet.[1] How many times do we desire the "meat" of the Word of God when we haven't processed the basics yet?

So the *Hebrew Writer in chapter 5 verse 11* tells them about Melchizedek, "Of whom we have many things to say and hard to be understood, seeing you are dull of hearing." Then he proceeds to the things they should understand but yet do not. In *Hebrews 5 Verse 12*, "For when you ought to be teachers (yourselves), you have need that one teach you again the first principals of the oracles of God, and are become such as have need of milk and not of meat (solid food).[2]

For everyone that useth milk is unskilled in the word of righteousness, for he is a baby. But solid food belongeth to them that are of full age, even them who by reason of use have their senses exercised to discern between good and evil." Hebrews 5 Verse 14 is our key text.[3]

The Power of Plain Words

Words contain the purpose, the destiny of the one who speaks them and the object spoken to, for they are the authority of man on the earth. While their power may be unknown to the speaker yet all of heaven's angelic hosts, as well as demonic spirits await the words through the authority of man to activate them. While most of the Church world is settled forever on the sovereignty of God ruling the universe; they have little to no understanding of man being given sovereignty on the earth in *Genesis 2 and 3*.[4]

As a result, man has become the victim of his own delusions. Man is often seen as the puppet of demented satanic forces or of a benevolent all wise God. In either case he is seen as lacking the strength or the power to resist either God or the devil.

True we allow a modicum of free will; otherwise salvation would be the act of God with or without our choice. This form of theology is no longer accepted by most nor is it an accurate interpretation of the Bible.

The history of everyone could be traced through words spoken to him and by him if we could accurately recover them. The Scripture declares that a man will give an account of all his productive and nonproductive words.

Whether they are negative or positive, predictive or non-predictive; words are endued with creative power. They have the power of incorruptible seed; they will bear fruit unless uprooted or rejected. Why such power and authority? Because all words, sounds, verbs, adjectives, adverbs, vowels are made audible by my breath passing through my mouth, tongue and teeth.

My breath can be thought of as my spirit. Out of the abundance of the heart the mouth speaks. My spirit is expressing itself with words that are the authority of my will, my sovereignty in and on the earth.

Understanding the Word of Righteousness

Every Israelite who knew the Torah and temple protocol desired to learn about this mysterious *Melchizedek* who appeared to *Abraham* and received tithe of him and who pronounced great blessings on Abraham. Who was he and where did he come to know the unknown (then) *Jehovah?*

Paul was saying the waters of such knowledge are too deep for you to navigate now. The most basic truths were not understood by these new believers. They didn't understand the *word of righteousness* yet. This is the most basic truth from which all other truth receives its impetus.

If you don't understand that you were made instantly righteous when you believed on Jesus Christ, you will always have a skewed view of every doctrine in the New Testament. You will never consistently use your faith for your fundamental needs; much less will you use them for the supernatural experiences with the Father God.

The sense of guilt and unworthiness will render you passive and immobile when action is required. So, you begin here as told in *2 Corinthians 5: 21.*"For He (God) made him (Jesus Christ) to be sin for us (in our rightful place), who knew no sin, to be sin, that we might be made the righteousness of God (his rightful place) in Him."[5]

The young immature mind can hardly grasp the fullness of such a staggering statement. This is our foundational truth; being as righteous as Jesus we have access to everything he has access to. We walk in divine favor. How many of us go around clouded with guilt about sins already forgiven and by God forgotten?

We can see that so much error concerning performance and being are covered with so much misunderstanding. Actually, we as parents have little expectation for performance in a 2 or 3-month old baby.

While in the Church we find so many who expect instantaneous perfection and maturity from newborn babes in Christ. We are not saved by works but our works are because we are saved. We bring forth works that demonstrate our repentance.

Aligning Our Minds with the Foundation of Truth

So, beginning with the foundation of all truth for Christian life we can now proceed to the solid food. How do we demonstrate that we are now mature enough to eat meat? By filling our minds with renewing words from the Word of God till our bodies and minds come in alignment with our spirit to judge all things.

Before you go off on a dialogue concerning judging, first find out what judgment is indicated.

1. Are we judging to indict as criminals against God and truth? [6]
2. Are we judging to discover truth and error?

The Greek word *dokimadzo* is a thoughtful word that means to "prove with the intent of approving."[7] The word was used of assayers who tested gold and silver with the motive of determining how much gold or silver was to be found in the ore being tested. This judgment is not to be feared or rejected by any of us. Something wonderful happens to us when we thus begin to discriminate before we accept or reject things that are brought to our attention in life.

This is the way we become well established in doctrine for Christian behavior and action. When God's will and ways are thoroughly founded in our hearts and minds, the body itself will have an autoimmune system to error and will automatically move into the realm of the Spirit.

Your Spirit having the preeminence will be the first to lead your soul and body into a rigorous training program for God's leadership and direction. We will no longer be led about by every wind of doctrine and the cunning craftiness of men. Simply for a man to be charismatic in personality and charming with his words is not enough for us to follow.

He or she must be sound in the *Word of God.* All truth begins in God's Word and only casts light on that Word so it may clearly be seen and understood. So the acclaim of man and what he teaches is to align what is being spoken with the Word. There are those who speak of the price they paid to receive their gift. Frankly, I differ; how many righteous deeds are needed to produce the gifts? The gifts never qualify the man, only the God who gave them can do this.

Should they be exercised by godly men and women? Absolutely! But sadly they often are not. For instance, the 13th chapter of *1 Corinthians* establishes how love should surround and cover every gift of the Spirit so no gift should come under justifiable condemnation.[8]

Sadly, the weaknesses of the vessels used by God are so often evident. Does that make the gifts any less wonderful and needed? No! It only demonstrates the graciousness of our heavenly Father to use whatever vessels are available to get mercy and love to us.

After all, how many holiness pills are necessary to produce healing or any other miracle? The gifts and their operation do not depend on our performance; else we could boast of our ability not God's grace.

12 Steps to Training Your Spirit to Discern Good and Evil

Let us look more closely at *Hebrews 5 verse 14.* The mature ones have trained their senses (sight, smell, hearing, taste, and feeling) to discern between good and evil. There are truths contained in this verse so profound that they were little known much less understood by the Body of Christ as a whole. They are unknown because there is little or no teaching on the subject.[9] Let's attempt some understanding of the truths presented.

1. Solid foods require a more mature digestive system than that of a small child. A baby eats predigested food (milk) that is easily redigested by them. Even as they progress the baby food is of soft, strained foods to introduce more sophisticated foods into their system as they grow.

2. The solid food (meat) is for the more mature ones who can now discern and assimilate deeper truths. These mature ones by receiving and understanding then train the senses to discern good and bad.

3. The mind, the soul and the psyche with all its parameters, develop a spiritual mind-set that is in like turn transmitted to body, bringing the body into the control of the spirit.

4. Correlate all this with *Galatians 5: 17-21*, the ignoble list of the sins of the flesh, which we charismatics have mislabeled as demonic; when actually the demonic has built up strongholds in our senses as an entryway into our carnal minds, thus controlling us and driving us further into bondage. No doubt Satan will attempt to use our senses to control and shape our destiny.[10]

5. There is an inner man (my spirit) that has spiritual senses that duplicate the physical senses. The skillful use of the Word of God will enable my spiritual senses to unite with my physical senses in discerning good and evil.

6. What is the gift of *discerning of spirits* but a revealing to the spiritually trained senses the things it apprehends? It is manifested in either a seeing of the spirits or a strong sense of those spirits.

7. The *word of knowledge* occurs when the Spirit in us opens the archives of divine knowledge, the past events and even the present that is hidden to us at the moment and suddenly we know that we know that we know. We know both the plans of God and of Satan. What has happened outside our ability to know both past and present to give us proper direction to a blessed event?

8. The *word of wisdom* is God's predetermined will and is immutable and inexorable in its march to fulfillment (this is God's sovereignty in action.) That word is transmitted to us so we can align ourselves and our doctrines to it in cooperation with God and His Purposes.

9. All the gifts of the spirit are manifested through our spirit, soul and body. All three have to align properly to manifest the gifts.

10. Healing gifts are transmitted usually by laying on of hands, by proclamation or by intercession (by known or unknown people in prayer.)

11. The gift of *tongues and interpretation of tongues* by definition require a human physical manifestation through human agency.

12. So also the prophetic gift, although the manner in which the gift is received may differ, the manner in which it is expressed is the same. It is either spoken or written; or both means are exercised.

The Holy Spirit is a spirit and must have a human body to use for Him to have legal access to the world. The same is true of demonic spirits to operate. *Galatians 5: 19- 21* show how Satan uses the flesh as his access point to take dominion over our lives. That access point (our flesh) and our words can give him legal right to try to destroy us.

Satan used the body of a serpent in *Genesis 3: 1-6* to tempt

Eve in the garden. Before we judge her too harshly, remember that she had never heard a lie, never had she met deception, while we often walk boldly into error knowing fully that it is wrong.[11]

So in connecting these passages we can see that our flesh and mind are the entryways which once used (either by God or the devil) can become strongholds. Think of it; my body becomes the entryway for every possible good of conversely every possible evil. The vast expanse of opportunity that is open to one human life staggers the imagination.

The Result of Training Your Spirit with the Word of God (Answered Prayers)

Do not think for a moment the apparent delays to answered prayers is in itself an answer. Just, wait awhile. For the Scripture says, "Hope deferred maketh dry the bones." Arthritis, rheumatism and neuralgia result from deferred hope. The timing of God is always perfect, "In due time Christ was born." When is the due time of my prayer request? What are the factors for receiving answers?

These questions receive ready answers in the Word of God. First, pray the will of God. What does that mean? Find the Scriptures that fit the desire of your prayer, that is the will of God. In finding the promise of God that describes the answer to your need. It also assures you of the will of God. All the promises of God in Christ Jesus are yes and amen. No one has a right to pray a prayer contrary to the will of God. Balaam the prophet found that out to his dismay.

Second, release your faith when you pray. Matthew 11: Therefore I say to you, whatsoever things you desire, when you pray, believe that you receive them and you shall have them." It is the height of foolishness to pray for something you desire but do not believe you will receive. Why bother? That is an exercise in futility. It is insulting to God.[12]

Third, the next verse set the protocol for answered prayer, "When you stand praying, forgive. If you have anything against anyone that your Father also, who is in heaven, may forgive you, your trespasses." This verse has been misinterpreted by many. They have taken the position that once you have been forgiven you can be then be unforgiven and as result lose your salvation.

Let us look carefully at this verse to arrive at its true meaning. Let me be clear in stating God does not give forgiveness and then take it back as the result of our subsequent actions. What is it that God cannot forgive but unforgiveness itself! I can never get past the unforgiveness at this point of my life till I return and forgive.

All answered prayer stop here at the point of my lack of forgiveness. All spiritual development stops at that place; all restoration stops at the moment I enter Gods prerogative of revenge. More than that, I am given into the hand of the tormentor, Satan and his demonic instruments of torment.

All healing and health, physical, emotional and spiritual are bereft from me till forgiveness is given. So if your prayers are not quickly answered check to see if lack of forgiveness is the reason for the blockage. The question is so vital the Father will not leave you without a quick answer.

Fourth, make warfare against the devil's forces for here is where the problem lies not with God. God is not trying to withhold blessings from you. Satan is! Attack him with spiritual prayer and put the force of faith to work against him. Satan would keep every prayer from being answered to destroy your will to prayer and to receive from God.

Putting a Face On Doctrine

Mary Todd Lincoln helped produce an Abraham Lincoln; while Mrs. Schicklegrubber produced an Adolph Hitler. In Oklahoma, a woman held in her arms a child of Indian heritage who would bring healing to thousands and establish a College (Oral Roberts

University.)

Has your body become the dwelling place of the Holy Spirit? Then who can put a limit on the potential contained within you? I urge you to train your body to operate in the spiritual gifting dormant within you. Release yourself from fears of failure and rejection to become the spiritual dynamo God has ordained you to be. Remember the hidden treasures in you are the Gifts of the Holy Spirit; your body is merely the vehicle that delivers those gifts to the world.

While you should treat the body with the respect it deserves; the greatest thing is the gift it contains. No wonder the Apostle Paul in *Romans 8: 22* declares "For we know the whole creation groans and travails until now" awaiting the "Adoption" the *hiosthesia* (the installation of us as mature adults in the Father's Kingdom)

That dear friend is not only our calling but our destiny. It is not only possible but inevitable when we grow in the grace of our Lord Jesus Christ. When we have trained our senses to discern properly when, how and where to ACT in accordance with God's leading, then and only then will the world be affected by our lives.

If you know the voice of the devil better than you know the voice of God, then you are not yet mature in Christ. Are you still asking the opinions of a dozen others before you seek the opinion of The Word of God? Then you still have some growing to do. At least seek the advice of someone who is mature in God and the things of God.

Chapter Notes:

1. Hebrews 5:12.
2. Hebrews 5:11, 12, 13.
3. Hebrews 5:14.
4. Genesis 2, 3.

5. 2 Corinthians 5:21.

6. Romans 12:1

7. *Dokimadzo* means to prove with the intent of approving. W.E. Vines Expository Dictionary of New Testament Words.

8. 1 Corinthians 13.

9. Hebrews 5:14.

10. Galatians 5:17-21.

11. Genesis 3:1-6.

12. Matthew 11.

CHAPTER 7

TRAINING YOUR SPIRIT WITH THE HOLY SPIRIT

As for you, the anointing you received from him remains in you, and you do not need anyone to teach you. But as his anointing teaches you about all things and as that anointing is real, not counterfeit—just as it has taught you, remain in him. —*I John 2:27*

CÆ

Prophecy Notes:

☐ Learning From the Holy Spirit (Himself)

☐ The Process the Holy Spirit Teaches

☐ All Believers Have the Mind of Christ

☐ Praying In the Spirit

☐ Producing the Dream by the Spirit of God

☐ Putting a Face On Doctrine

Through the years I have been a student searching for information in the books and libraries at my disposal. The problem in seeking Biblical knowledge is that you are left with the business of weeding out incorrect information of the personal ideologies of the one writing. Were they prejudiced by their theological background or the doctrinal teaching of their particular denomination?

For many, they are focused on a particular paradigm

that did not allow them to accept teaching that contradicted their particular belief system. Just look at most of the Bible commentaries on the Holy Spirit's baptism. They are strangely silent or in outright denial of the evident practices of *Acts 2:4*. Why is this? [1]

Because such practices are foreign to their adopted doctrines, they may know that their experience of God is genuine but doesn't include the experience of speaking in tongues. Therefore, the baptism of the Holy Spirit with speaking in tongues must be either false or false.

Learning from the Holy Spirit (Himself)

So where do we go to find the answers to the many mysteries that confront us in knowing? I suggest that we need to do as the early church which had no New Testament at its inception. We must learn from the Holy Spirit himself. The Spirit, who breathed the inspiration into every New Testament writer for every word of their Epistles is the perfect interpreter for His own message.

In *Acts chapter 2* men spoke in 16 different languages and prophesied of the wonderful works of God. The Apostle Peter gave the marvelous Pentecostal message under the anointing and direction of the Holy Spirit. Yet, here we are 2000 years later trying to improve on Gods original plan by looking to men to direct us to shortcuts on understanding God. [2]

Listen to the directives from the lips of Jesus to his befuddled disciples in *John 14:26* "But the comforter, who is the Holy Spirit, whom the father shall send in my name, he shall teach you all things, and bring all things to your remembrance, whatsoever I have commanded you." [3] And in the continuation of the same message in *John 16: 13*, "Nevertheless, when He the Spirit of truth is come, he will guide you into all truth; for he will not speak of himself, but whatsoever he shall hear, that shall he speak; and he shall show you things to come." [4]

The Process the Holy Spirit Teaches

Note the process the Holy Spirit teaches and guides. That process includes taking the commandments of Jesus which are written in the gospels and the epistles; in other words the Scriptures remind us of what we already know but may have let slip.

Then further, He takes us into uncharted territory and guides us into territory he is well-acquainted with: hearing the voice of God and showing us things to come. In showing us things to come, this is not just prophetic insight into world events but much rather insight into Gods prepared things for us and the lives of our loved ones. (I will deal with this more fully in just a little while.)

The teaching excellence of the Holy Spirit is further highlighted in *1 John 2:2*. "But the anointing which you have received of him abideth in you, and you need not that any man teach you; but as the same anointing teacheth you of all things, and is truth, and is no lie, and even as it hath taught you, ye shall abide in him."[5]

First let us lay aside our fears that this verse opens the door to all sorts of goofy off-the-wall doctrines and ridiculous theories. The Holy Spirit in-breathed every word of the Holy Scriptures and he will not be a party to any adulteration of that record. There are those who try to wrest the Scriptures and put their own "spin" on them. They do so to their own peril.

The Holy Spirit is totally integrated and congruent with himself, with the Father and with Jesus, they are one. In a simplistic view, he is telling us the indwelling Spirit set up a classroom in our spirits as our pedagogue to train, equip, and guide us to the fulfillment of our chosen purpose. I entertain the knowledge of his indwelling presence by doing what he has spoken into my spirit.

In *1 Corinthians 2* the entire 16 verses contain many unexplored and untaught revelations that are relevant to our hearing the voice of God for us. In this chapter the great Apostle makes some revealing statements about himself. One is that he has come to them with divine revelation of wisdom that is backed up with the power and demonstration of the Holy Spirit.[6]

This powerful assertion literally states he came with overwhelming proof that demanded agreement as provided by the Holy Spirit. Yet even with such authority and power he came in weakness and much fear and trembling. (He doesn't sound like a great Apostle here.)

What was he fearful of? Was he fearful of personal attacks, physical or spiritual, hardly? (He was fearful that the Corinthian church would refuse his message and his mission to them would be lost or irreparably damaged.) So he casts aside all previous knowledge of them acquired by personal ministry among them and determines to know nothing about them but Christ and Him crucified.

From this point, he begins a treatise on how to know mysteries about people especially from 1 Corinthians verses 9-16. But as it is written, Eye hath not seen, nor ear heard, neither have entered the heart of man, the things which God hath prepared for them that love."[7]

At this point most traditional people stop and begin to exclaim about the beauties of heaven and the glories that await us. However, I submit to you that heaven is not the subject of discussion. Rather, the Apostle Paul is discussing heavenly wisdom and understanding, where it comes from and how to get there!

Read the next verses: 1 Corinthian 10-16. "But God hath revealed them unto us by his Spirit; for the Spirit searcheth all things, yea, the deep things of God. For what man knoweth the things of a man, except the spirit of man which is in him? Even so the things of God knoweth no man but the Spirit of God. Now we have received, not the spirit of the world but the Spirit who is of God; that we might know the things that are freely given to us of God. (Listen to the proclamation of that verse!)[8]

We already have within us the ability to know the things

freely given, things prepared for us. They are not being withheld from us; they are being held for us! "Which things also we speak, not in the words which mans wisdom teacheth, but which the Holy Spirit teacheth, comparing spiritual things with spiritual. (Here the apostle describes the change of language; it is freighted with spiritual significance, leading men to a new understanding of spiritual truth. The physical is not to be compared with the spiritual; they are two different realms.

ALL Believers Have the Mind of Christ!

"But the natural man receiveth not the things of the Spirit of God; they are foolishness unto him, neither can he know them, because they are spiritually discerned. But he that is spiritual judgeth all things, yet he himself is judged of no man. For who hath known the mind of the Lord, that He may instruct him? But we have the mind of Christ."

Can you begin to see that we (most of us) have gone around confessing ignorance and then wondering why we were ignorant? The great Apostle Paul makes a startling declaration that includes ALL believers. We have the mind of Christ! We have an anointed mind, a spiritual mind that is capable of discerning and understanding spiritual things.

That inside us, in the spirit man, is the compendium of knowledge needed to supply me with all grace for my particular destiny. The Father has graciously prepared for me the graces, gifts, and abilities to reach my purpose in life, successfully. The next question is how do I tap into these resources?

I believe that one of the most effective resources lies in the ability to pray, worship and praise with tongues. I do not say these are the only ways to tap into the spirit realm of the Father.

But I do unequivocally declare that speaking with other tongues is a tremendous facilitator for revelation knowledge and perception! *1 Corinthians 14: 2*, "For he that speaketh in an unknown tongue speaketh not unto men, but unto God; for no man understandeth him; however in the spirit he speaketh mysteries." Two tremendous facts are stated here.[9]

First, the man or woman who speaks in tongues speaks to God. James chapter 5 declares that if God hears us we have the petition we have asked of him. So step one not only assures me that I have an audience with God but that what is prayed in the Spirit is answered.

Second, another problem arises: however in the spirit he speaks mysteries. *W.E. Vines, Expository Dictionary of New Testament Words* tells us the word translated mystery is the Greek word: *Musterion* meaning that which is outside the range of unassisted natural apprehension, can only be made known only by Divine revelation and is made known in a manner and at a time appointed by God and to those who are illuminated by his Spirit. In the spiritual sense *musterion* is truth revealed.[10]

Let us investigate this truth of mystery a little deeper. The mysteries are not mysteries to God who knows all things; He is omniscient. I am praying things in the spirit that are mysteries to me. (Initially, I may be ignorant of my calling, my purpose and my destiny. Until, little by little clues begin to appear. I begin to feel a gentle tugging inside me for new passions about things that at one time did not interest me.

Sometimes the drawing of God becomes almost unbearable in its intensity. A sudden knowing arises that seems as if it always existed; it is there in my innermost being. Face it friend; you have just heard the voice of God concerning the things which he hath prepared for you.

Revelation knowledge becomes all consuming knowledge that can never be doubted again. Remember, in all this apparent mystery God wants you to know the answers. Without the answers you will never reach maturity or the purposes of God for your life. God never reveals all the answers ahead of time, only as we need them and have developed the maturity to enact them. It is a walk of faith, a process to grow to the fullness of that which God has designed.

Relationship is the result of several factors: proximity, communication, caring, and sharing. The element of worship establishes proximity. I enter his gates with thanksgiving and praise but I enter the Holy of Holies by worship. I submit that praying in tongues gets me into the presence more quickly than any other way.

For prayer in the Spirit by passes the ignorance and the arrogance of the mind. My spirit coupled with the Holy Spirit cuts to the heart of issues beyond my natural understanding. *Romans 8:26,* "Likewise the Spirit also helpeth our infirmity; for we know not what to pray for as we ought; but the Spirit himself maketh intercession for us in groanings that cannot be uttered." Further, Romans 8:27 "And he that searcheth the hearts knoweth what is the mind of the Spirit, because he maketh intercession for the saints according to the will of God."[11]

In these verses we have all of the requisites of relationship: proximity, communication, caring, and sharing. Closeness to the Father is more than a feeling; it is the awareness that I am one with the Father irregardless of the emotions of the moment. It is that unity that makes me realize that my will has become his will. They are now one and the same. (In much the same way a man and wife act in unity though physically apart because of their unity with each other.)

Praying In the Spirit

In all relationships communication is the key to begin and to maintain the relationship. It is much more than the words, for words can conceal as well as reveal. There are those who chatter incessantly but never say anything; while another may say one word that conveys tons of emotions and information.

There is not a formula that declares instant success, if you pray for such and such a length of time. The book of James uses Elijah as a model for prayer on Mount Carmel yet his prayer is covered in two verses of scripture in *1 Kings 18:36-37*. Sixty two words in all; but with words that shook heaven and earth James then declares the fervent prayer of a righteous man avails much.[12]

How much have your prayers out of your natural understanding accomplished? Try praying in the Spirit. So, out of this vast reservoir of opportunity comes the vital method of communication with God, my spirit in communion with my Father. In that secret place of the most high I share a gracious time of fellowship. It is from this special place that I learn the secrets of God and He speaks His individual will for my life. An inner knowing of the direction and purpose fills the vacancy of ignorance.

Again, I do not suggest that praying in tongues is the only method of knowing God and His will. Other methods such as meditation, study, worship and opening the heart in understanding prayer are available to all. Whatever the method, the important factor is to develop the relationship!

Pastor Ron Phillips of Abbas House in Chattanooga, Tennessee has written a book titled "Secrets Of The Stairs" based on *Songs Of Solomon 2:14*. The invitation of the bride groom to his beloved to climb the secret stairs (steps cut in the mountain to get to the heights up steep places. It is much like the Hopi Indians who lived in the cliffs of the Rocky Mountains.) This he couples with *Psalms 91: 1-16*. Psalms 91 verse one boldly declares, "He that dwelleth in the secret place of the Most High shall abide under the shadow of the Almighty."[13]

It is significant to note that every blessing that follows in the remaining verses depends on doing verse one: dwelling and abiding in the secret place of the Most High. The choice to dwell and abide is entirely at our discretion. I can make myself at home with God! Can anything be more desirable? Living with God; oh happy thought this is my place of invulnerability. It is the place in my life that Satan cannot invade nor attack.

How can I hear the voice of God? Get close enough to hear. Stay close and open the ears of my spirit to hear. Once I have heard the voice of my Father remember the sound and quality of that voice so when I hear it again I will recognize it immediately.

Once I have established the sound of His voice I will be able to hear it with confidence and trust. There are many voices that I do not recognize, but the voice of my Shepherd I do know and obey; I will not follow the voices of confusion and error. The more I hear the voice of God, the more He will speak to me. I know as He shared with Adam and Eve in the cool of the day so will he share with me the secret of His prepared things for me.

What the Scriptures enjoin is a lifestyle of living in constant communion with the Father. Developing an awareness of His voice, this is much more than a mystical experience which occurs on an occasional basis.

God desires our constant fellowship until we know Him as Abba Father (Daddy God); I do not mean a disrespecting attitude but rather a normal child father relationship of closeness. God doesn't want to live in miracle relationship with us always but one of mature children respecting and honoring the position, power and place of the Father, in which the supernatural is normal and comfortable for us.

The supernatural is the expected and normal range of our experience with the Father. Now as a mature one in the Fathers house, I can expect to receive daily communication from the Spirit on how to use Divine wisdom for the benefit of the family. Such wisdom may astound others but has become the normal pattern of thinking as I dwell in the secret place of the Most High God. This is our daily walk.

There is nothing about it that seems supernatural except the amount of anointing that rests on me to deliver the messages of truth I receive. Sometimes the urgency of the message overwhelms the spiritual emotions and energizes the body and mind to astonishing reactions beyond the normal. As Jesus told his disciples "I have meat to eat that you know not of." Come into the Fathers house and share this exciting journey!

Producing the Dream By the Spirit of God

When? That is the question that prefaces most of our questions with prophecy and dreams. We are grandly stirred with emotions when we first hear or see the promise of a wonderful future. Quickly, however, we come to the place of interminable waiting; the enthusiasm wanes and the vision dims.

"What can we do" and "What should we do" in the meantime? It is in the meantime that faith is tested in the fiery furnace of impatience and a million questions that enforce the impossibility of the promised future. The fetus of the dream may bear resemblance to the infant to be birthed. Wait for the process to be completed. It is worth the wait.

What should we do meanwhile? After the heart conceives the dream, pregnancy takes place. The time of pregnancy is the time when tremendous changes take place in the body. There are not only physical but emotional changes that are part of the mystery of birth. This is also the process in the spiritual realm when the birth of a dream is anticipated.

Changes in the person so honored by the Father must take place for them to fulfill the dream. Spiritual growth to maturity is necessary for the dream to achieve its fullest purpose. The patient waiting of faith and hope is not a fatalistic whatever will be, will be. The expectant parents of a child prepare clothing, bedding, and room for the child to be. And all the while give special care and attention of the producing mother.

Likewise, in the waiting room for dreams promised, the mother of the dream is fed on the Word of God, exercised by obedience and nurtured by prayer to maintain good spiritual health. This is not God's responsibility; this is ours. So in the domain of faith, the dream is grown to full term so it can maintain life after birth.

The insemination of the dream is only the beginning point of the dream that previews the future. It is not the arrival at the destination! The dream is intended to motivate us to move toward the dream and to provide direction and purpose to our lives. Move towards your prophecy and dream.

Begin the initial steps of preparation to fulfill your destiny. Do you need more knowledge of your intended dream? Saturate yourself with all the information you can find on the subject. Do not neglect the spirit man! Immerse him in spirit activity and develop the relationship you have with the Father.

Avoid as much as possible the "comfort" of Jobs friends, a veritable sea of accusation and condemnation, disdain and denial of your right to the dream. You can't always choose your enemies but you can choose your friends.

Surround yourself with believers, ones who will support you whether they understand your vision or not. The world is filled with abortionists who are embittered by the death of their dreams and do not want yours to succeed as a testimony to their failure. Their lack of vision, hope and faith has been the death knell of countless opportunities to bless the world.

There comes a point when pregnancy is apparent to everyone. The physical changes signal the baby is coming to term. As the expectant mother has taken proper care of herself and the coming child, the body itself knows the proper time to begin the birth process. The beginning of travail signals to the mother it is time. Finally to be able to see and hold in the arms the product of the 9 months of gestation; oh what joy!

Different dreams require a different time of delivery. Generally, the larger the dream the longer the time of preparation it will require. The greater the building the deeper the foundation to support the edifice envisioned must be. Small dreams may be realized quickly. However that fact may lead to self-satisfied smugness that looks down on those who are still producing their greater dream. Accepting average is the destruction of the dream of excellence. Excellence requires greater effort and constant vigilance. Mediocrity requires only the ability to copy others, producing the boxes of sameness.

The first requirement of producing the dream is to accept

ownership of the dream. The vision is mine; God gave it to me. It is my responsibility to do; it is mine. I have no greater purpose than the vision of my dream. The mother to be has almost the sole burden of carrying the baby to term.

The father is almost an insignificant bystander in this delicate operation. His bonding to the child usually comes after the birthing not before or during. Even so, completing your dream is more up to you than it is to God! God has already revealed His will to you by giving you the dream.

He has placed in your hands the textbook for fulfilling dreams, the Bible. It is filled with promises of provision and how to receive that provision. *Isaiah 66: 9* says, "Shall I bring to birth and not cause to bring forth? Shall I cause to bring forth, and shut up the womb?" All power has been given to you to exercise the plans of God on the earth.

After ownership the next step is to declare your faith in the ultimate accomplishment of your dream. State your faith again and again till there is no room for doubt and fear to intrude into your consciousness. Maintaining faith and trust is besieged on every side by mountains of doubt and assailed by fears, but take heart dear one; faith and trust will bear precious fruit.

Understand that your dream is not just for your well-being but has an intention to benefit the world. The dream that includes only you is much too small and is not the goal that God intends.

It is meanwhile that God is developing the person who is carrying out God's greatest objectives in you. He is growing the person of you from your baby first steps to the maturity of whom you should be.

So, don't allow criticism to dam up the streams of creativity that flow from the belly of believing ones. Act like a winning one who is already basking in the sunlight of success. Act as if the dream were already achieved. Declare things that be not as though they were.

That is the formula and a principle of success. From time to time, step back and view the progress made. Has the path been followed in a straight line? Or have you deviated from the vision originally received? If so, correct your course to its proper direction. Focus on the goal!

You who have received the vision, a word of prophecy, a dream of purpose are the blessed ones. You have seen the Promised Land; the direction of your life is distinct and well-defined. There is no longer mystery about your future. The broad outlines of your destiny wait only the paintbrush of the colors of your choosing to paint he picture of your life and its destiny.

Trust the support of faith to withstand the barbs of rejection, denial and antagonism to carry you through to victory. Isn't it amazing that we believers can have no problem believing for our future home in heaven but are awed at the prospect of believing God for earthly provision now? The dream and hope painted the picture for faith to fulfill and faith rushes to reward the dream.

The dreamer must become a doer. Many dreams die of inertia and lack of momentum. Surround yourself with faith images. It is not so much that faith is fragile, rather that it is wasted time to spend life listening to negatives that can over the passage of time erode the vision and distort the dream.

I will not allow my focus to be altered and momentum of the dream to be dissipated and drained of energy. I refuse to allow myself to drown in the sloughs of self-pity or despondency.

Thus I am involved in a great enterprise that brings me in contact with all the enabling abilities of God to walk into my land of promise. Let us venture forth into the success of our dreams. Milk and honey await the investment of our time and energy.

Putting a Face on Doctrine

In the most traumatic times of my spiritual experience, times when I was overwhelmed with the sense of defeat and discouragement, my only recourse was praying in the spirit. Then, I did not know the power of praying in tongues. I would often say the only thing I had going for me was that I prayed in the spirit. As if that was a small matter.

Praying in the spirit is never a small matter. It can change worlds and mine did. I was praying myself into the will of God as I prayed mysteries. During my prayer, I became aware that my family and I were moving to South Carolina, why, I did not know; how, I did not know; I just knew we were going.

This was the gift of a word of wisdom, God's predetermined will. It was there that a whole new ministry of prophecy had its inception. An understanding of spiritual leadership came to me from new sources of teaching. I stayed with a charismatic Bible study that enriched me a thousand times over. I believe that I prayed myself into these developments by praying the mysteries in tongues. Everything did not come into perfect alignment overnight; but a process was begun.

In the night times of my distress, I sang songs in the spirit that sounded like funeral dirges. These melodies solidified my resolve to face life with optimism. Defeats were turned into victories; battles were won that I never have to fight again.

One particular experience became one of my first enlarged occurrences of prophecy in my life. I took my oldest daughter from Augusta to Kannapolis N.C. to visit her cousins who lived there. On my return trip, I began to sing a simple little song in the spirit when suddenly the spirit of prophecy came on me and for the next eighty miles I prophesied about the plans of God for the Augusta, Georgia area.

I said things in the privacy of my car that I would have had difficulty saying to anyone else. As Jessie Duplantis said, "When you are alone and you prophesy you have no difficulty in knowing to whom you are prophesying." The up building of that moment carried me through many trials and tests.

In recent years the Lord has given me poems which are spiritual songs unsung. The encouragement embodied in them has dried the tears of many. They have recounted to me how uplifted they were in dark moments by a song of the spirit.

Sing songs that uplift and motivate you to worship and to

action. Some of the most powerful songs I have ever heard were sung by me in the Spirit and were never heard by others. They were my personal songs of joy and victory. They built me up on my most holy faith.

Chapter Notes:

1. Acts 2:4.
2. Acts 2.
3. John 14:26.
4. John 16:13.
5. I John 2:2.
6. I Corinthians 2:16.
7. I Corinthians 2:9-16.
8. I Corinthians 2:10-16.
9. I Corinthians 14:2.
10. *Musterion* meaning that which is outside the range of unassisted natural apprehension, can only be made known only by Divine revelation and is made known in a manner and at a time appointed by God and to those who are illuminated by his Spirit. In the spiritual sense *musterion* is truth revealed. *W.E. Vines, Expository Dictionary of New Testament Words.*
11. Romans 8:26, 27.
12. I Kings 18:36-37.
13. Songs of Solomon 2:14; Psalms 91:1-16.

CHAPTER 8

ACCELERATING YOUR GIFT OF PROPHECY

Let the word of Christ dwell in you richly, in all wisdom teaching and admonishing one another in psalms and hymns and spiritual songs singing with grace in your heart unto the Lord —*Colossians 3:16*

C3

Prophecy Notes:

- ☐ The Progress of Prophecy
- ☐ Accelerating Your Gift of Prophecy with the Word of God
- ☐ Accelerating Your Gift of Prophecy with Prayer in the Spirit
- ☐ Accelerate Your Gift of Prophecy with Building Up Yourselves
- ☐ Accelerate Your Gift of Prophecy with the Spirit of Deja Vu
- ☐ Putting a Face On Doctrine

This is the time of rapid fulfillment of prophecies and promises. Events are being compressed by the *kyros* (strategic times.) times. Knowing the times of divine purpose is essential for the prophet to have credibility. The world is being flooded with nebulous promises obscured with religious jargon.

It is not enough to prophesy great things. It is time to accompany the prophecy with faith. If you don't have faith to produce it, don't prophesy it! The credibility of the prophet is tied to results that are tangible!

It is not enough to produce heightened expectations or to enflame the emotions to ecstatic responses. Expectations unfulfilled result in anger, frustration, bitterness and eventually active unbelief, both of the prophet and of the God he speaks for. Inflamed passions without realization leave the spirit in disappointment that wallows in hopelessness.

Do not prophesy beyond your ability to believe. How can one prophesy in faith? By knowing the accuracy of the word you have heard. Then release your faith from the heart with the words you have heard. When you know that you have heard the voice of the Father then you can have confidence that God's ability under girds the words spoken.

So, child rise out of the desperation of your fears, for the light of the completed promise changes the dark days of fruitlessness and blessing. Rise to the new level of joy for you will speak seed to many nations.

The Progress of Prophecy

Changes, changes, changes! This is the constant cry heard in the Church. Father, change this! Dear Lord, change that! Yet when change comes they cry to return to the comfort zones of the past. All changes are not evolutionary, some are revolutionary.

Israel left the bondage of Egypt to wander on the deserts of the Sinai. The desert provided little to sustain life (even a camel had to carry a six-to-eight day water supply in his hump to make it.) The desert experience required total dependence on God to sustain six million Jews daily. Only angelic ministry could perform such a task.

In like manner this "world" has nothing in it to sustain spiritual life. We must eat the manna, the living Word and walk the walk of faith daily to receive our life support from heaven.

As changes are the inevitability of life, we must learn to adapt to new challenges and new situations. In the same manner to grow spiritually, I must leave the status quo to secure new victories. I must choose the adaptation of repentance for old thinking, the willingness to have a teachable attitude and to leave bad doctrines behind.

The doctrines in and of themselves were not necessarily evil but were tainted with a slight bending of truth (the perversion to doctrine is often subtle almost imperceptible and therein lies its danger.) Why changes? There are changes because the Apostle Paul declared we are being changed from glory to glory.

In other words the change is from one state of good to a higher good so greater good can result from our lives. Thank God I am not what I was, I am what I am, but I am not what I will be!

There is a change in the atmosphere as spiritually electric forces build up to magnum intensity. As the days of this age progress to fuller revelation, they require a greater responsibility to respond to the revelations received. The changes needed to accommodate the plans of God have taken on urgency for time is quickly moving to the culmination of all things.

As we see the integrity of the Father, the promises of God are being fulfilled around us. The things of the invisible world are rapidly being manifested in the visible realm to be clearly seen.

As the marvelous plans, promises and purposes of God with indisputable evidences certain changes will take place. These undeniable proofs will either change the rejections of mere human reason or result in hardened hearts of unbelief. The agnosticism of some will become the rage of those whose bastions of humanism and atheism are swept aside by the revival of faith and the renewal of the Church's authority within the state.

The strongholds of sexual lasciviousness will fall before a new understanding of life's purpose. The stronghold of abortion which had its inception in the doctrine of sexual liberty will bow to the call for the sanctity of all life to be honored and respected. The shrines of intellectual dominion will be shaken as the indisputable proofs of God's truths are established by archeology and other scientific discoveries.

The main impediments to the Kingdom rule will be defeated by the spiritual conquest of the uprising of the church to establish Kingdom authority. First it will happen in the church itself then in the world around us. Few territories will accede to the reign of our Father without battle that ends in conquest. Even where it seems the enemy is joining us by seceding their territories to us; beware of the Gibeonites whose hypocrisies led Israel to preserve them as they were annexed to Israel's power.

The army of attack is even now being marshaled to bring about enormous changes. Strongholds will be crushed into rubble. The Church which has for so long been in a circle with the wagons mentality will awaken to discover that it can deal crippling blows to the enemy. The full armament of the Holy Spirit that resides in our spirit equips us for constant victory.

The effective use of prayers that attack the strongholds of demonic power will at last become aggressive weapons that win and root out the defeated foe. (For too long we have seen prayer as the last resort, maybe it will work, all else has failed.) As a result, we prayed faithless prayers that were never heard by the Father and so never answered.

The only prayers that we as confessing Christians have a right to pray are prayers according to God's will. (His Word is his will.) Our quiver is filled with faith arrows to shoot at the enemy. Words spoken with authority will bring death to Satan's dominion.

We have the nine gifts of the spirit in our arsenal that protect us from Satan's invasions but also propel us to defeat him in his own territory. All of these precious gifts are inherent in believers to extend the rule of the Kingdom. What king would send his troops into battle without all the necessary equipment to wage a successful war?

All of heaven waits in breathless wonder; when will the church arise in power and use the armament that God has provided? Heaven can and will do nothing till man (reborn man) exercises the power and authority God has given him. Jesus Christ the prototype showed forth the authority when He the firstborn rose from the dead conquering death, hell and the grave, by exhibiting salvation's perfect redemption.

God has left the greatest task to us, the reborn ones, that of Evangelization of the entire world, establishing kingdom rule on the earth. Can you see it? Will you do it?

Prophecy Note: Expand Your Vision

The closer to the ground one is determines the extent of the boundaries one is capable of seeing. The limited vision keeps one in self-imposed paradigms of what happened yesterday and what is happening today and all that from a narrow perspective of me, mine and sometimes yours.

To see clearly you must climb the mountains above the tree line, above the lower elevations of foot hills and small mountains, for the panoramic vision of wide range and full revelation of Gods plans for tomorrow. Climbing to the heights is not the minimal efforts of most of the Body to climb upward.

There are risks involved in mountain climbing that put the climber at peril with little or no apparent help. The first is the loneliness that is intrinsic with the undertaking itself. Few people are willing to undertake the journey. You may be called on to blaze new trails to places where no other foot has trod. This is not the journey for the weak, trembling spirit.

Your desire and faith must rise to their highest level, and maintain that high level of competency despite rejection, ridicule, and accusation. Those weaker ones you left behind on lower levels will hurl many threats and accusations against you. They will speak of your pride as the motivation for your passion to climb to the limits of finding favor with God.

They will declare loudly every flaw in your character, both real and imagined. In so doing, the covering of the Church is removed exposing the true prophet to all-out kamikaze attacks from Satan and high-level demonic forces who always come in multiple numbers with hideous devices to attempt the defeat and destruction of the prophet.

So climb if you must but do not go with innocent unawareness of the enemy's devices. You do not wish to be found in the most dangerous moment of your climb with just a slender handhold on the next level of progress; and suddenly find yourself under your greatest attack.

The Boy Scout motto comes into play; be prepared! Send your prayers and prophetic proclamations in advance. Get the promise of victory before the battle. Know where the ambushes and traps have been laid and assign your prayers and prophecies to them with the full assurance of victory before the fight is enjoined.

So the climb for the heights will not only bring solitude but clear vision as well. Remember in climbing the mountain it was not for you alone that you came. It's true you desired communion and fellowship unhindered with the Father. More than desiring fellowship, you desired knowledge and wisdom for the people of God. For many of whom are bound in chains of addictions, limited relationships and virtual ignorance of the freedoms and powers that lie within their grasp.

So climb you must for the destinies of multitudes lie in your pathway of vision and proclamation. To further the Kingdom is in your hands to either expedite or to impede.

When you are on the highest peaks you will find little to sustain you. Did you bring all the necessary food and equipment to maintain you for the period of time you will be there? You will not live forever on the peaks but you have found the secrets of how to get there again and again.

Once the mountain has bared its bosom to you; it is yours to conquer again and again. Now that your have seen the heart of the Father you have standing invitation and knowledge of how to find the secret place of the Most High. The effort, the tears, the toil were not wasted, despite the critics and rejecters; you have spoken and given birth to what you saw.

Have you reached beyond the desire to have acclaim and

approval? If not, you stand in a place for manipulation and control by satanic forces. You are destined to be a mouthpiece for God; seek no greater accolade than that.

So climb the mountain to its highest point attainable for this insures the widest most penetrating vision possible for you. You now stand where few men have gone. In the fearful days of your beginnings you saw only the closest things around you but now you are the eyes and ears for thousands.

Faint not at the task before you for like Joshua of old you are living in cities you did not build and eating of vineyards you did not plant. You have only now begun to reach the beginnings of the potentials of Kingdom harvest. In all that you do I will establish MY NAME and MY KINGDOM.

Accelerating Your Gift of Prophecy with the Word of God

Ignorance is inexcusable when we have a written document that contains all the relevant material we need to have a relationship with Father in both Spirit and Truth. Your knowledge of the Father will be limited or blemished without knowing the God of The Word. It is amazing the distortions that have proceeded from the lips of preachers and teachers because of their incomplete knowledge of the Word.

Do not allow your prophecy to be inaccurate because of your unwillingness to study. Study requires effort and diligence to arrive at the place of being able to divide rightly the Word of Truth. Study becomes the lifelong commitment for anyone who desires to become a workman for God.

The Scripture alluded to is, 2 *Timothy 2:15*.[1] It has the Greek word *spoudazo* translated as study when the better word would be <u>give diligence</u> which means to hasten to do a thing, to exert oneself, give diligence. This is far more than merely reading the Word.[2] There are people who read the Word but do not have an understanding of the Word they read.

The Ethiopian Eunuch who was reading from the Prophet Isaiah of whom Philip inquired, "Understandest thou what thou readest?" Because my striving to learn is to gain Gods approval. It is one of the means by which I reach maturity; I go beyond the milk stage of a baby to being able to eat and digest meat or solid foods. The level of our ability to process grown up diet is a sign of Gods approval for us to move on to deeper things.

Also, the purpose for study is to be able to divide rightly the Scriptures. The Greek work *Orthotomeo* is to cut straight.[3] What is intended is not dividing Scripture from Scripture but teaching Scripture accurately. (W.E.Vines, for example.) Knowledge of God is foundational to spiritual growth. The Apostle Paul in *Hebrews 7* lamented the fact the churches he was addressing who should be teachers had not grown up enough to teach and required someone come again and teach them the first principals laying foundations not building on the foundation.[4]

The distortions that are seen in some church bodies is the direct result of a lack of spiritual development by the church leadership. They major in minors and become specialist in a form of doctrine without developing a full and varied program for growing up the church in all aspects of maturity.

We must never establish the precedence of experience over the word. To do so is to bring total anarchy and chaos. It is to destroy all boundaries and structure and to leave the church to drift into reefs of self-destruction.

Accelerating Your Gift of Prophecy With Prayer In the Spirit

The Apostle Paul sets the standard for ministerial practice in *1 Corinthians 14: 14-15,* "For if I pray in an unknown tongue, my spirit prays, but my understanding is unfruitful. What is it, then? I will pray with the spirit and I will pray with the understanding also; I will sing with the spirit, and I will sing with the understanding also."[5]

Let us gain understanding of what the Apostle Paul is saying, for it will enable us to follow the same rule of spiritual conduct. There are two choices of the manner of prayer extended to every Spirit filled believer. There are prayers from my natural understanding in my native speech.

These prayers while valuable depend on my knowledge of facts or events, and my ability to verbalize them. The only limits of this kind of prayer are my knowledge of the will of God and my understanding of the apparent need. The maturity of my experience with the Father or lack of it may hinder the deeper needs that are unknown to my natural understanding.

So the Apostle shows us the remedy in *Romans 8:26*, "Likewise, the Spirit also helpeth our infirmity; for we know not what we ought to pray for as we ought; but the Spirit himself maketh intercession for us with groanings which cannot be uttered." What is the infirmity?[6]

Paul identifies the weakness and failure as ignorance of the real needs. We don't know what to pray for as we ought. That lack of knowing has hindered the effectiveness of our prayer lives many times over. We have prayed for the superficial or the unnecessary and then were puzzled by Gods ignoring our righteous pleadings. See the comparison of my knowledge (your knowledge) with the knowledge of God.

There is no comparison to be made. So why would I choose my knowledge over His? That is beyond pride; that is arrogance of the highest order. Notice again the Apostle Paul declares in verse 18, "I thank my God, I speak in tongues more that you all." We know that Paul didn't disobey his own injunction about speaking in tongues in the church except with certain parameters on them.[7]

So where and why did he speak in tongues at all? If tongues were merely gibberish or the ravings of a mad person, why would the apostle boast of his lingual proficiency? Consider the reasons involved for his claim. One, the great Apostle needed edification after and before all the physical and vocal abuse he received in his apostolic ministry.

Two with the physical and emotional stress from his enemies, He carried the spiritual weight of the Churches he helped birth in Asia Minor and Greece and finally in Italy. These infant churches required his constant care and instruction to keep them from error and eventual destruction.

Three the care he exercised demanded supernatural wisdom and knowledge to have effective results. No wonder he prayed in the spirit so much. Apostles and Prophets pay attention so you are always connected to your source of help.

Not only the fivefold ministry but all believers arm yourselves with praying in the spirit as often as desired and needed. You don't have to wait for a spiritual urging. Paul said I will pray with the spirit; I will pray with the understanding also. We should choose to do the same.

Praying in the spirit demands a certain kind of discipline because the mind is not involved in the prayer. As a result, the mind will wander form thought to thought without regard for their spiritual content. You may have a thousand mundane thoughts while you are engaged in praying in tongues and come under guilt because of such thinking.

You may even wonder what good is praying like this while my thoughts are so carnal? Don't despair; the mind will eventually come under control during this meditation and God thoughts will arrive. Revelation is activated by praying in the spirit. That revelation will be in several areas.

What is the will of God for my life? What is the answer for specific needs in my life? What are the needs for others for whom I am praying? What and for whom am I praying? (Many times I am making intercession for unknown people and their particular needs). By praying and singing in the spirit I am building myself up on my most holy faith.

To construct that most holy faith will be essential for meeting the struggles of tomorrow. Are you tired of meeting problems and dealing with them after the fact? Wouldn't it be nice to deal with the problem before the damage required complete restoration?

How does this apply specifically to prophecy? I believe that everything that has been written is applicable to prophecy.

Does prophecy require spiritual knowledge and understanding? Absolutely; not only to receive the word needed, but how to speak that word effectively to the receiving one.

The manner in which I speak the prophecy may be as important as the message that is given. Tongues of prayer are an expediter of the gift. What do you do when you have blank moment in the exercise of the gift? Praying in the spirit can bring immediate results in receiving then in delivery of the message. To receive a word for me is one thing; to receive a word for someone else is quite another.

To receive for me, may require no speaking of it at all. To receive for another requires that I verbalize it either in speech or by writing it. Once we confirm by faith the message is accurate and timely; we then go immediately with courage and confidence to deliver that word in the appropriate manner.

The whole process is often started by paying in the spirit. This can be done in many ways; praying softly under your breath as a whispered prayer in public (church, home, hospital or anywhere where loud praying would be unacceptable). As a matter of fact, the loudness of any prayer is not necessarily a sign of anointing and effectiveness. Faith produces results not my emotional state. When you have properly edified yourself then you are equipped to fulfill your ministry.

Accelerating Your Gift of Prophecy by Building Up Yourself

Being the go between of God and man is a tremendous responsibility and places great emphasis on the critical care of my relationships both with God and with men. God ward, I must not allow anything to interrupt the relationship with my heavenly Father. He is a covenant keeping God who will never renege on his word. The Father will keep His promises regardless of my behavior. His Word is established forever.

However, there will be constant attacks from demonic entities to disrupt my relationship with the Father. My prayer life will be overwhelmed by disruptions and the interference of daily activities. My study patterns of learning God's Word will necessitate discipline. There are acts of discipline that I must be accountable to initiate myself.

Of all the disciplines in the world, self-discipline is the most vitally needed by all of us. *Ephesians 5:18-21*, "And be not drunk with wine, in which is excess, but be filled with the Spirit. Speaking to yourselves in psalms and hymns and spiritual songs, singing and making melody in your heart to the Lord, Giving thanks always for all things unto the Father in the name of the Lord Jesus Christ, Submitting yourselves one to another in the fear of God."[8]

And in *Colossians 3:16*, "Let the word of God dwell in you richly, in all wisdom teaching and admonishing one another, in psalms and hymns and spiritual songs singing with grace in your hearts to the Lord."[9] Then my third corroborating witness is found in Jude verse 20, 'But ye beloved, building up yourselves on your most holy faith, praying in the Holy Spirit."[10]

Using these texts as a touchstone for personal edification, let me state in clear terms that you will never edify others unless you have first been edified. In becoming a spokesperson for God, you become the critical reason for ministry in the Spirit. If you are weak in faith or deficient in the word you will minister out that weakness or that ignorance.

God can only minister truth to me as I maintain a teachable spirit with quickness to repent for traditions and accept new revelation. I am not talking about supplanting solid doctrine with false revelation. I am referring to revelation of the Word.

For instance in *Ephesians 5:18-21* Paul in context is dealing with specific problems faced by the churches in Ephesus, that of dealing with their walk and behavior as newborn ones to the faith. They are warned to flee from their former life styles that were characterized by fornication, uncleanness, covetousness, filthiness, or foolish jesting.[11]

How are they to accomplish this new attitude? They

accomplish it by being constantly filled with the spirit. How do they maintain constantly being filled with the Spirit? They are constantly filled by speaking to yourselves in psalms, hymns, and spiritual songs, making melody in your heart praising God and submitting to one another.

These are the secrets of personal edification that will carry over to my life with my wife and family and into the outside world. Don't ask God to do what He has placed in your hands to do. The tools are in your hands to bring all the strength you need for every occasion. God won't build you up while you sit on the stool of do-nothing whistling the tune of do-less.

There is no provision for spiritual laziness. I have heard Christian people complain of the lack of spiritual food in their local church. I say, "Well grow up and feed yourself." The Bible on your lap has enough food to supply you with all the nutrients you need for a lifetime. You are not a baby any more.

The letter to the Church at Colosse tells us how we can supply the needs of others. We can help supply the needs of others by singing psalms, hymns, and spiritual songs, singing with grace. As my songs of praise and adoration and worship of the father flow forth to the ears of others they are built up by my ministering to them out of a built up spirit.

In your study of the Colossian letter you will discover that they were being bombarded by false teachers who would bring them under spiritual bondage to meats and drink, feast days and new moons and even the Sabbath day observance. The remedy for these intrusions was to be built up on their most holy faith. To be so edified would give them an unshakable foundation.[12]

Jude provides further amplification in verse 3 of his short epistle. "But ye, beloved, building up yourselves on your most holy faith, praying in the Holy Spirit." Jude was written when false teachers and false prophets were making an onslaught against the churches that Jude oversaw.[13]

In the most graphic of terms, Jude saw the need for the believers to whom he wrote to take special precautions. Not just pray but pray in the Holy Spirit to fortress yourself against these pernicious enemies of the faith once delivered to the saints. Praying in the spirit is a deterrent to false doctrine and error.

After all, He inspired every word of the sacred page. He has been commissioned to teach and reveal the message of God to us all. Again there is no justifiable excuse for being misled into false doctrine. I can assure you that you will have to ignore all the influences of the Holy Spirit to go wrong.

In every mistake you have made in decisions since you have been born-again you were warned ahead of time not to do so. But because you relied too much on the wisdom or charisma of a preacher or teacher you let their influence overcome your checks from the Holy Spirit.

Or possibly you got spiritually lazy and let others decide for you. Or it is probable that your desire for things beyond the will of God drove you to disobedience. But you have within you the tools to avoid failure or error. Build up your spirit to hear the inner voice of God. He will speak to you and establish you.

Accelerating Your Gift of Prophecy by the Spirit of Deja Vu

The advantage of seeing or hearing from God in a prophetic revelation is that as you walk into your future you are constantly meeting the spirit of "deja vu." Deja vu, a French word meaning "already sean" or expressed as a funny feeling that you have already done something before or met someone before, even though this is the first time.

The fore-knowledge says that I've been here before. That knowledge provides us with knowledge of what to expect (both from God and from satanic influences.) That prior knowledge comes to us in dreams and visions and words inside our spirits so we can meet every obstruction with assurance of victory.

I know the exact result of my obedience to the message clearly received. So, informed I have a clear purpose that leaves no excuse for failure. I have seen it before. I know how much dedication is needed.

I know how much commitment is required. My spiritual eyes and ears have revealed it all. From all this divine information is birthed a steadfast faith needed to reach the desired goal. The prophetic word allows no tremors of fear and unbelief. The word that we have received is a "sure word of prophecy."

The ambushes of the enemies of the prophet Elisha were always revealed to the prophet ahead of time.[14] Jesus himself said in *John 5:19*, "...verily, verily I say unto you, the Son can do nothing of himself, but what he seeth the Father do; for what ever things He doeth, these also doeth the Son in the same manner."[15]

So the pattern is set for us to follow. We know what to do, when to do and how to do for we have already seen ourselves doing it! We know in advance whether to fight, who to fight, and how to fight. No nation goes into battle without a battle plan.

Yet, the Church of the Lord Jesus Christ constantly goes into warfare with the battle plan that is from yesterday, led by war weary generals who have no contact with the warfare of today and outdated armament.

Oh believer! We have secret weapons in our arsenal that outgun the enemy in every conflict we will ever face. We are stationed at strategic points not merely for defense but for offense as well. We have spiritual weapons that have been erased from Satan's memory.

He has no understanding of spiritual matters for he dwells in darkness and darkness cannot comprehend the light. There are things we need to do without talking about them "Ad Nauseum". Just do it!

I refuse to become one who merely talks a good game. I will be a doer of the Word of God and escape the trap of self-deception. Talk only without action is to be self-deluded and rendered inoperable not having any ability to battle the enemy successfully.

Putting a Face on Doctrine

There have been times when I was faced by someone who needed immediate answers to problems far beyond my ability to comprehend, much less supply. However, after a brief prayer in the spirit, the answer that came was both simple and doable.

The *word of wisdom* or *word of knowledge* unlocked what seemed both mysterious and having no answer. In counseling with people who were so entangled with emotional storms of anger and rage, a few quiet moments of praying in the spirit quieted the storm and peace came again so solutions were found and situations were resolved.

When I was counseling in Augusta, Georgia I was confronted with a young woman who was suffering extreme panic attacks. She was calling 911 every few minutes; since there was no physical source for her problem they had no solution.

Sitting in front of me while she was describing her situation I was praying almost silently, when suddenly I saw the root of her problem; she had been sexually molested in her childhood. Exercising extreme caution I was able to bring her to resolution in her difficulties.

Especially when prophesying to several people in a row, you may have to refresh yourself for new or a renewed proficiency to prophecy. First you do not want to fall back on prophetic catch words "You are moving to a new level." which means absolutely nothing without describing where that new level is or where it leads. To avoid giving repeat prophecies, pray in between each person as needed to keep your prophecies fresh and accurate.

Relationship is the vital component of prophecy. Times too numerous to count, I have met with insurmountable difficulty only to have them evaporate with an amazingly simple answer from the Holy Spirit, when I prayed in the Spirit.

Chapter Notes:

1. 1 2 Timothy 2:15
2. *Spoudazo* – study. *W.E. Vines, Expository Dictionary of New Testament Words.*
3. *Orthotomeo* – cut straight. *W.E. Vines, Expository Dictionary of New Testament Words.*
4. Hebrews 7.
5. 1 Corinthians 14:14-15.
6. Romans 8:26.
7. Romans 8:18.
8. Ephesians 5:18-21.
9. Colossians 3:16.
10. Jude 20.
11. Epesians 5:18-21.
12. Colossians.
13. Jude 3.
14. 2 Kings 6:4.
15. John 5:19.

CHAPTER 9

SPEAKING PROPHECY WITH EDIFICATION

Do not let any unwholesome talk come out of your mouths but only what is helpful for building others up according to their needs, that is may benefit those who listen. And do not grieve the Holy Spirit of God with whom you were sealed for the day of redemption. —Ephesians 4:29, 30

ॐ

Prophecy Notes:

☐ The Mandate of the Fivefold Ministry

☐ Edifying Yourself by Praying In the Holy Spirit

☐ Edifying Others by Praying In the Holy Spirit

☐ New Testament Prophecy & the Word of Grace

☐ Grace! Grace! And More Grace!

☐ Putting a Face on Doctrine

The next three chapters are the heart and soul of New Testament prophecy. They explain the content, purpose and protocol for all prophecy in the local Church Body. It is worthy to note that until the first book of Corinthians was written there were no regulations or explanations of how prophecy was to be conducted.

To me the wonder is not that there were erroneous practices

in this early Church but that there were not many more even more egregious ones than those mentioned in 1 Corinthians 14:26. "How is it, then brethren? When you are come together, everyone of you hath a tongue, everyone of you hath a song, hath a doctrine, hath a revelations, hath an interpretation. Let all things be done unto edifying."[1]

Take notice the Apostle did not say anything negative about what was sung or said either in doctrine or revelation! Rather he called attention to behavior and practice; do only those things that edify. Attention without the perimeter of blessing and benefiting those in attendance was prohibited. The Apostle Paul dealt with the order and motivation of the expression of the gifts.

The Mandate of the Fivefold Ministry

There's a mandate given to the fivefold ministry. Number one, the perfecting of the saints is more literally for the maturing of the Saints. Maturity is the process of growth till the product is complete, whole, and ripe (as a crop ready to harvest). This sounds like an extended process to me. Childhood may be remembered as a joyous carefree period; but ask any child what is his or her dream and they point to their desire to grow up and be big.

Every area of our lives cries out for growth. Physically, the body demands our best effort to protect for renewal and for good health. Intellectually the mind and spirit are in a lifelong search, not just for information but understanding of the information received.

Emotional maturity is essential for the person to assess the events in their lives with proper responses. My younger brother made a statement that impressed me then and still does. "Being mature doesn't mean that I am always right in my decisions, but it does mean that I take responsibility for my decisions." At another time, he said something equally impressive when asked what was the most important thing he brought to his pastorate? He replied, "I bring emotional maturity." Thanks, Wayne.

To that response I would add spiritual maturity and faith based intellectual maturity. I declare on this basis, without the fivefold ministry, we would forfeit maturity in the Church.

Second, for the work of the ministry, literally every program of the church is to be carried out by those who have been equipped by the fivefold ministry and empowered by the Holy Spirit. Missions (both home missions and foreign missions), all charitable works, and every facet of the work of the church needs the building blocks supplied by this God given assistance.

One needs only to look at the early history of America where every university and every hospital was founded by the church. This fact is sadly ignored by our politically correct society. As a matter of fact, the first widely read primer of all Americans was the McGuffy Reader.

It was more responsible for literacy in America than any other single book and it was chiefly the Bible rendered to simple terms. The single most important reason in producing the work of the church is strengthening the fivefold ministry.

Edifying Yourself by Praying In the Holy Spirit

Jude, the brother of Jesus, in his short letter even gives an outline of self-help for all believers. In *Jude verses 20-23*, after warning of false prophets, false teachers and apostasy, he declares: "But you, beloved, building up yourselves on your most holy faith, by praying in the Holy Spirit, keep yourselves in the love of God, looking for the mercy of our Lord Jesus Christ unto eternal life. And on some have a compassion making a difference; and others save with fear, pulling (snatching) them out of the fire, hating even the garment spotted by the flesh."[2]

Those who despise tongues as a manifestation of the Spirit must have a problem with this text. For if one is against the manifestation of tongues, I think its either ignored or focused on other parts of this verse. Jude is urging the believer to pray in the Holy Spirit. I must confess in my early Pentecostal experience

I interpreted praying in the Holy Spirit as praying with a spirit of prayer.

I would become almost frenzied with loud pleading (I sounded more like the prophets of Baal than I did the prophet Elijah.) Oh, how I tried to impress God with my zeal and earnestness. Jude says build yourself up by praying in the Holy Spirit. I will now make some bold assertions:

1. The amount of revelation knowledge you possess in directly in proportion the amount of time you pray in the spirit.

2. The power level of your life and ministry (both dunamis and exousia) is also directly responsible to prayer in the Spirit.

3. This praying in the Spirit is a facilitator for all the gifts of the Spirit.

4. The mysteries referred to in 1 Corinthians 14:2 according to W. E. Vines, are things which are: "outside the range of unassisted natural apprehension, can be made known only by Divine revelation...its Scriptural significance is truth revealed."[3]

Isn't it amazing the very gift that apparently caused so much trouble in the Corinthian Church is so highly valued by Jude? No, not really, Jude recognized where and how the gift could be used to its greatest advantage. Let us follow his advice and example. Build up ourselves. Don't wait for others to do the job, you and I should do.

May I be blunt? "Quit sucking your thumb in self-pity and inaction. Build yourself up on your most Holy Faith. It's your job." It has been my experience that many Pentecostals have never spoken in tongues since their initial infilling; while many others have to have an overwhelming emotional experience to engage in this vital practice. I cannot imagine a day without communion with the Father in my prayer language.

Do not suppose that because revelation is not instantaneous that it is not coming at all; you may need to grow in your spirit to receive the knowledge that God wishes to give you.

You don't begin to erect a structure at the top floor first.

Allow the revelation to come in its time. Jude was not apparently fearful of weird off-the-wall revelations. He specifically says that when you pray in the Spirit you are building yourself up on your most Holy Faith.

Fellow believer the Holy Spirit is not conflicted; nor does He have a split personality. He is always consistent with all revealed knowledge. He has an excellent memory.

Edifying Others by Praying In the Holy Spirit

The revelation knowledge received will help keep you in the love of God. Believe me this is no small task. To keep a loving attitude when all hell is breaking loose around you requires many moments of praying in the Holy Spirit.

Indeed, the only way that you can bring yourself to love some people is to spend time praying in the Spirit (and most of those are people in the church.) Notice, that he then says we are able to make a difference and have compassion, snatching some from the fire, while with great fear, we wonder if it is possible to reclaim them.

What is the difference? We can see that their sin is of the flesh; it is not a character flaw. There are some sins that are unto death; others are redeemable. How do I tell the difference? That's why you are praying in the Spirit. You dare not rely on your flesh judgment! Read *Galatians 5:19-21* about the works of the flesh.[4]

Do not misunderstand me; all of these works of the flesh will do damage and lead to eventual character flaws and distortions that can make you unfit for Kingdom service. Here again is the enormity of our task to snatch them from the fires of fleshly passions.

And all the while, we hate even the stench, the awful bad smell of the flesh spotted garments. This is not a hating of the person or people who are involved in the works of the flesh. It is hate for even the smell of spotted garments. The Greek word for spotted is interesting: *Spilas* has two different translations in *Jude, verse 12*, speaking of false teachers, calls them spots (Spilas in this context means hidden reefs or rocks that can imperil a ship at sea.) [5]

Then in Jude verse 23, "spotted garment" at first glance it may appear a miss translation. Yet, on further examination the same danger is enjoined in the danger spots, rocks at sea, and moral failure spotting. It's the same danger as the self-righteous clothing of Holy appearance that would cause shipwreck in the lives who continue to leave undealt with works of the flesh.

Now Jude did not recommend the beating into insensibility those involved in the works of the flesh. Why? They are redeemable. Snatch them out of the fire even if it is uncomfortable to your sensibilities. Love reaches downward and horizontally to save erring brothers.

Jude then reminds them that our keeper cannot only keep us from falling but presents us faultless before His glory with great joy. The list of the works of the flesh is both long and infamous, "Adultery, fornication, uncleanness, lasciviousness, idolatry, wrath, factions, seditions, heresies, envying, murders, drunkenness, reveling, and the like.

The continued practice of these works of the flesh will result in closing the doors of the Kingdom within you that hold love, joy, and peace in the Holy Ghost. So fellow traveler look out for the hidden reefs, the Holy Spirit knows where they are, let him pilot you to the safe harbor of your final destiny.

In closing, *Chapter 4 of Ephesians, verse 29* says: "Let no corrupt communication proceed out of your mouth, but that which is good, to the use of edifying that may minister grace to the hearers."[6]

Two words stand out that we need to define: First, **corrupt**, in the Greek *Phthiero* meaning to destroy by bringing into a worse state by corrupting.[7] The danger is of bringing the church (individually or collectively) into a worse state.

New Testament Prophecy and the Word of Grace

Second, **communication** meaning *Logos*, a spoken word that expresses the sum total of my attitudes, ideas, and concepts (my personal definition, take it for what it's worth).[8] So, the Apostle Paul says don't allow those words that demean or make lesser of people.

Rather, only speak words of grace. (Consider the illustration I gave earlier with Bartholomew prophesying to my son-in-law about contracts he would have the opportunity to sign that would be injurious to his God given dream. There was no accusation or undue pressure attached to his admonition plus he planted the seed that a better contract was coming.

After much wrestling with the flesh Tim obeyed the prophecy and the second contract came and it was better. The warning was given in love not a demand for unqualified obedience to the prophet.)

All the reference to comfort, edify, and exhortation in *1 Corinthians 14* leave no room for negative, accusative, judgmental prophecies. Listen to the Apostle Paul pray for the elders of the church at Ephesus in *Acts 20:32*, "And now, brethren I commend you to God, and TO THE WORD OF HIS GRACE, which is able to build you up and give you an inheritance among them that are sanctified."[9]

The word of grace is the pattern for all our speech to one another. The very best prophecy is the Word of God itself. You cannot err when you cite the Word of God, the perfect remedy for all the ills of the church collectively and individually. The built up believer then has a heritage among them that are sanctified.

What an august company to live in association with, those who are separated unto God; not just separated from sin but vitally connected for Gods service. Oh to be at His beck and call for immediate use. I share with *Isaiah* the hot burning desire "Here am I Lord; send me", I am already prepared and established for your call and commissioning. Such is the power of gracious words! Are you calling people to the destined place, the place of God's grace?

Grace! Grace! And More Grace!

Grace did not come into being because of sin. Grace is the redundant superfluity of agape love, the very nature of our heavenly Father. Grace is the glue that holds together all the multiplicities of God's attributes. It is the balance wheel the keeps unlimited power and unbridled wrath from destroying everything sin touches.

Justice and mercy are met and man is enfolded in that embrace. How marvelous are the tender mercies of our God. Moses asked to see a physical revelation of God but was only allowed to see the hinder parts of God. Isaiah saw the Lord high and lifted up and His train filled the temple. The train was the trail left by the bride's gown.

I might say the hinder parts of God. God showed them both what they needed to see as described in *Exodus 34: 6 and 7*. The glory of God was much more than a cloud of *Shekinah*, It was a trail of mercies and tender love faithfully rendered to a faithless people.[10]

Moses saw the goodness of God pass before him with its many facets of forgiving mercies in full revelation. The march of mercy began before the foundation of the world with a crucified savior. From the Garden of Eden to our present-day the lightning flashes of grace appear.

The true voices of the spirit ring out with anthems and hymns of the deepest emotions of man the recipient of grace. The inner man who has been bathed in the warm glow of mercy's healing rays cries out in unutterable groans of delight.

Those who have never sung such a song of joy have yet to taste the power of forgiveness and the beauty of His person. If once seen the altogether lovely one, nothing compares to such magnificence. What diamond or gemstone could call forth such adoration, such worship, such love! Jesus the light of heaven evokes the praise of angels and men.

Jesus contains all the perfections of the Father and embodied them in full measure. Eternity's glory will forever be exhibited by Him through us, His Body, for angels and seraphims to observe and wonder at such manifested grace. We the redeemed are the crown jewels of grace and mercy, Jesus, the beauty of all ages: past, present and future.

Jesus is our logos and our Rhema, the full revelation of the Father and the individual bursts of personal revelation. He is my all in all. Grace, grace, grace!

Putting a Face on Doctrine

I have prophesied to many people; I have been blessed with responses by those who declared that they were uplifted, encouraged, and pointed in the right direction. There have been those in the grieving process for rejection, reviling, abandonment and yes grieving from death's separation, who have reported a new lease on life, hopes rekindled, destiny established because a word of prophecy was given.

So I have been encouraged by the Holy Spirit to continue the ministry gift of prophecy. Because a prophecy unspoken, dies aborted in the birth chamber without ever seeing life. From my heart and lips have come the only affirmations some have ever heard. And I only repeated what I heard in my spirit.

What a treasure to be the one allowed to apply the healing balm of Gilead to wounded suffering ones. What accomplishment in life could be greater than that? You have been placed in the position to minister in the place as a substitute Jesus, who always ministered in love.

Chapter Notes

1. I Corinthians 14:26.
2. Jude 20-23.
3. *Mysterious* – Outside the range of unassisted natural apprehension can be made known only by Divine revelation. *W.E. Vines, Expository Dictionary of New Testament Words.*
4. Galatians 5:19-21.
5. *Spilas* – Hidden reefs or rocks that can imperil a ship at sea. *W.E. Vines, Expository Dictionary of New Testament Words.* Jude 12.
6. Ephesians 4:29.
7. *Phthiero* – corrupt meaning to destroy by bringing into a worse state by corruption. *W.E. Vines, Expository Dictionary of New Testament Words.*
8. *Logos* – Communication meaning a spoken word that expresses the sum total of my attitudes, ideas and concepts. Charles Rosson.
9. Acts 20:32.
10. Exodus 34:6, 7.

CHAPTER 10

SPEAKING PROPHECY WITH EXHORTATION

And with many other words, did he testify and exhort, saying save yourself from this crooked generation. —Acts 2:40

ભ

Prophecy Notes:

☐ Who is the Exhorter

☐ The Exhorter Apostle Paul

☐ The Exhorter Titus

☐ Giving Attention to the Word of Truth

☐ Growing Up to Exercise the Gifts Properly

☐ Putting a Face On Doctrine

Exhortation is perhaps one of the most misunderstood and little used manifestations of prophecy. It is not the art of criticism, nit picking or the exposure of the life of the one being prophesied to. The Apostle Paul gives an example of exhortation in *Acts 15-43* where he traced the history of Israel from Egyptian bondage up to his present day.[1]

After the death and resurrection of Jesus Christ, all this discourse is an act of exhortation. He spoke strongly yet it was lovingly urging them to receive Jesus Christ. Also, notice *1*

Timothy 5:1 says, "Rebuke not an elder but exhort (entreat) him as a father."[2] So, we see the pattern of exhortation is with tender words that exert tremendous power.

Who is the Exhorter

The word **exhortation** is from the Greek word *parakaleo* and its various derivations mean to sit down with, near to, to call alongside, to invite, to entreat, to pray for, and to cover alongside.[3] Also, it means to cover with a veil to hide. This word shows the closeness of fellowship. It is the partnership of loving caring, companionship saying I'm right beside you brother ready to come to your defense in an instant.

Brother I've got your back. If you need a boost, climb on my shoulders; I'm here to lift you over the fences that keep you from your dream. I will put a veil over your blemishes till they are corrected and your true beauty comes forth. I'm your back up, I'm your support and I'm in your corner. As the Holy Spirit is our *paracletos* and is committed to us forever, so are we committed to be the same for one another.

You don't lose my prayerful support because of any lapses in judgment and practice. I will always be there to say the best and believe the best of and for you. To do anything less is a failure on my part as a fellow believer. Because of our vital connection in the Body of Jesus Christ, a failure of one part puts the entire Body at risk.

A simple root of bitterness can be like an infection spreading rapidly with its contagion to impair the whole body. Just the root of bitterness allows the devil to attack whenever and however he pleases. The tragedy of bitterness and unforgiveness is that often the slight is more imagined than real. The exhorter is often a cheerleader, whose enthusiasm inspires to bring out the best in others. *Acts 2:40, "And with many other words, did he testify and exhort, saying save yourself from this crooked generation."*[4]

The phrase crooked generation is *to be bent out of shape.*[5] This was true of them both in attitude and action. In other words, the Apostle Peter had clearly outlined the gospel message of grace. Now he implores them to take the avenue of escape: follow Jesus Christ and His message. It is amazing how the message of exhortation comes with a seemingly untoward word in critical times.

Apostle Paul the Exhorter

In *Acts 27*, we find the Apostle Paul in the midst of the "perfect storm" on a journey he had advised against. After the experienced sailors had now despaired of life, in the middle of a hopeless situation Paul stands up to speak.[6] Now would be the perfect chance to declare: "I told you so. Nobody ever listens to me. It's all your fault; you dummy."

But no, that is not his response! He speaks, "And now I exhort you to be of good cheer…" Cheer up; the man must be mad or stupid! Here in the center of the winds of *euroclydon*, cheer up, it's obvious this man knows nothing of the doom we face.

On a personal level, have you had one of those people who never face reality; speak to you when all hell was breaking loose around give you those tremendous words that were supposed to solve your dooming situation with those trite words "cheer up"?

It made you want to smack them. But, Paul continued his statement with a solution and a reason for hope. In Acts 27 verse 23, "For there stood by me this night an angel of God, whose I am and whom I serve."[7] As the result of that visit Paul has received God's perfect plan for deliverance. I say to you in your darkest night of trouble, there are angels ready to minister assistance and aid with the perfect remedy for your life.

Titus the Exhorter

In the book of Titus is a pastoral letter to instruct a pastor on his duties as a minister to a church, namely to the church in Crete. The reputation of the population of Crete was horrible, citing a prophet of their own chapter 1:12-13 "...The Creteans are always liars, evil beasts, lazy gluttons." To which the Apostle adds: "This testimony is true..."

No wonder Paul in his introduction in verse two speaks of God "who cannot lie". Surrounded by the dark clouds of constant lies by evil beasts and lazy gluttons (It would be hard to love and care for such a graceless people; how could you have pride in such a group? There was a source of constant truth that Titus could flee to, the word of God).

Here child of God is your refuge from lies; God who cannot and will not lie? But how would you like to have to pastor such a group of churches? Yet even for people of such low character, there is hope. Read the entire 2nd chapter of Titus and the 3rd chapter as well, a total of 30 verses, for it is all exhortation.[8] <u>That exhortation involved teaching, encouragement, and equipping</u>.

1 Timothy 4:13, "Till I come give attendance to reading, to exhortation, to doctrine."[9] Then he urges Timothy "neglect not the gift that is in thee, which was given thee by *prophecy*, with the laying on of hands of the presbytery, meditate upon these things; give yourself wholly to them, that your profiting may appear to all. Take heed unto yourself and unto the doctrine, continue in them; for in so doing you will save yourself, and those that hear you." Pay attention to how the Apostle prioritizes things for Timothy to do.

Giving Attention to the Word of Truth

First, give attendance to reading (his only Bible was the Old Testament). Second, he is encouraged to attend to exhortation. The Apostle wrote two epistles to his son in the Lord to exhort him when Timothy was facing difficult times.

In addition, he gave him direction on pastoral matters and church leadership choices. Timothy had a problem with the place of women in the church, because he had been raised by women (his mother and his grandmother). He was disposed to relinquish his authority to them.

I remind you that you cannot compare the station of women in Paul and Timothy's day to that of today. The education of women is relatively new to the culture of the world. As recent as the early nineteen hundreds, it was considered a waste of resources to educate a woman, whose only future was to be a homemaker and to bear children.

I know that history gives the accounts of many educated women who made their mark in life; they were the exception, not the rule. I am not trying to negate women and am happy that times have changed. I am simply pointing out that many of the arguments about the attitudes of then and now are comparing apples with oranges.

Not only did he have that problem but many tried to run over-the-top of his authority. If you are in leadership, always know that some will try to usurp your authority. Don't get paranoid, but do recognize the dangers, so "Let no man despise your youth, but be thou an example of the believers in faith, in purity." [10]

The speed of the time change (daylight savings) is a prophetic wake up call to the Body of Christ, "It's later than you think." If your physical senses are accustomed to a certain pattern. It's time to change that pattern. You will be calling for the Lord to stop the moon in progress in the valley Aijalon; because more time is needed to conquer the enemy. You have heard the prophetic voices declaring acceleration and multiplication are for this season and the church.

This is God's time for *blitz krieg*, lightening warfare; are you ready to increase your service in the Kingdom? This is the day of constant attack. Hear well the voice of the prophets, each of them in their particular field, make a constant message to emphasize the need to run fast to keep up with the times.

It is time to prepare for the influx of people and churches that are looking to (your church.) It is here that much teaching and equipping the next generation for the times of today and tomorrow will take place.

Do not say that I need to relax and spend more time in leisure; nor will the Lord hear the pleas of limitation of time and talents. *Isaiah 40: 31,* "They that wait upon the Lord shall mount up with wings as Eagles; they shall RUN and not be weary, they shall walk and not faint. This is the day of an aggressive faith that is ready to pillage the camp of the enemy.[1]

The day of spending our time trying to refurbish those who refuse to grow and go are over. Those who demanded constant attention and have monopolized the ministry of the church without ever growing up must end. If pruning of the vineyard is necessary, then hear well the voice of the Lord, it will be done whether willingly or unwillingly! So if you hear groaning and weeping in the background learn to discern whether it's from real need or merely selfish attention seeking of those hard to maintain ones.

I am not suggesting we become hardened of heart but discerning of Spirit. This is not a day for coddling the permanently failing to grow. They will either grow up or be passed by. The day we are facing requires our best and most useful of service. It is time to deal with eternal issues. We are setting the standards of tomorrow. Let us develop and train our newborn ones. This is a priority that will take the most delicate of balance and attention of all leadership.

Prophecy Note: The Path to Destiny

The path to destiny is filled with seeming interruptions, pauses, and detours before one reaches their destination. All these delays obstruct my reaching my "high calling" and "royal purpose." As we consider these rest stops along the way, I would like to offer some explanations.

Even the greatest symphonies ever composed have included in them rest stops. Some of these rest stops are for intensifying the music to follow; others show a change of musical direction (new themes or different rhythms to follow). These pregnant pauses are the "Selah" (pause and think about this) that allow us to think carefully about the past before going on into the future. The rest allows us to bring forth the best of the music of life. The pause concentrates our attention on lessons that should have already been learned from yesterday's experiences that are the springboard for the "Grand Finale."

This is the time for studied reflection, to use the past as a learning tool that is the foundation for growth and success. Hopefully, the past also contained some victories; victories that inspire us as building blocks for the future. Samson stood at the carcass of a lion he had slain in battles of yesterday and found hands full of honey to sustain him in the present.

Yesterday's victories have sweet possibilities for today and tomorrow. The rest time is not for delay but as a time to replenish our strength and to reestablish our focus. The time of refreshment will energize us with renewed vigor and determination to reach for the impossible dream.

The rest stop will encourage us to meditate. A country preacher once described meditation as "Getting something good out of something you got good out of before." Essentially meditation is squeezing all the nutriments from the subject under consideration.

The pause will enable us to be led to hope, as life's experiences past are viewed from today's knowledge. With this added knowledge we can clearly see the divine purpose of God's inspired rest stop.

Now I can view the dream as my destined plan from God and declare as the Apostle Paul: "Forgetting those things which are behind, I press toward the mark of the prize of the high calling of God in Christ Jesus."

All of his past, good and bad were cast on the dung heap of discarded trash worth only to be burned in the fires of forgetfulness. The past, once I have gotten its lessons is nothing but baggage to anchor me in dead memories.

The dream within me is like a seed that pushes from the ground reaching forth to touch the sun's rays of life-giving warmth. The faith in me rises with acclamations, "I know whom I have believed." And knowing Him causes me to be able to wait patiently on the "whys", the "how's", and the "when's". All of my questions are answered in "knowing Him."

Growing Up to Exercise the Gifts Properly!

This is a study of spiritual growth, as seen in a New Testament word study. All the definitions of the Greek are taken from *W.E. Vines, Expository Dictionary of New Testament Words.* Using *2 Corinthians 13: 8-13* as a text:

"Love never faileth; but whether there be prophecies, they shall be done away; whether there be tongues, they shall cease; whether there be knowledge, it shall vanish away.

For now we know in part, and we prophesy in part. But when that which is perfect is come, then that which is in part shall be done away. When I was a child; I spoke as a child, I understood as a child, I thought as a child; but when I became a man, I put away childlike things.

For now we see through a glass darkly; but then face-to-face; now I know in part, but then I shall know even as I am known. And now abideth faith, hope, love, these three; but the greatest of these is love."[11]

Twice in *verse 11* the term child is used. Let us consider these definitions in the Greek for they show the process of growth toward manhood. The Greek language is more specific than is the English language. The English language uses comprehensive and inclusive words that are spelled the same way or pronounced the same way but have totally different meanings.

For instance the word bear; depending on its usage, can be interpreted to mean bear a burden or an animal such as a black bear. Or the word pronounced *bear* but spelled *bare with* means to be unclothed or naked. All that said, let us note the word child in verse 11. The Greek word *Nepios* refers to a nonspeaking child, a child who can't communicate in proper language.[12]

144

Romans 2:20 describes these children at this stage of life as those who are carnal not spiritually developed yet. Or as *1 Corinthians 3:1* as those who are partakers of milk because they are "without experience of the word of righteousness." Righteousness is the beginning point of salvation and they are still at the starting gate of Christian experience.[13]

Nephos is always associated with immaturity or the failure to develop to adulthood.[14] The Apostle Paul says there came a time when he left behind the things of childhood; being impressionable, selfishness, self-centeredness to become conscious of others around him. He became a man *aner* as distinct from a child but not just an *antropos* meaning a member of the human race, rather a distinct person among many men.[15]

The Greek language also defines a babe as a *brephos* meaning an unborn child (a fetus) or a newborn infant.[16] Take a look at these Scriptures with the Greek word *brephos*:

1. *In Luke 1:41 Elizabeth felt her brephos leap in her womb when she was visited by Mary.[17]*
2. *A newborn infant in Luke 2:12, "And this shall be assign unto you; you shall find the babe (brephos) wrapped in swaddling clothes lying in a manger.[18]*
3. *II Timothy 3:15, "And that from a child (brephos) thou hast known the Holy Scriptures which are able to make thee wise unto salvation through faith which is in Christ Jesus."[19]*
4. *1 Peter 2: 1-5, "As a child (brephos) desire the sincere milk of the word (that is desire the pure, without snare or deceit, word.)[20]*

Then the word child *paidion* is used to describe the development of a *nepios* one totally under the care and training of its mother to the hands of its father.[21] In Jewish custom a son was not responsible to keep the Mosaic Law until he was *Bar Mitzvahed* at age 12. In that day and age instant obedience from a child (Paidion) was expected. Notice the language in the following verse, "Suffer little children to come unto me, and forbid them not, for of such is the Kingdom of heaven."

At seven, the child was a *pais* till age 12. As a *paidion* or *pais* Jesus entered the temple to be about his Fathers business. *I Corinthians 14:18-20* set the parameters for those exercising the gifts of the Spirit. "I thank my God, I speak with tongues more than you all; yet in the church I had rather speak five words with my understanding, that by my voice I might teach others also, than ten thousand words in an unknown tongue.[22]

Brethren, be not children (*paidions*) in understanding; however in malice be ye children, but in understanding be men (*aner*) distinct from a child, mature. Grow up!

Yet another stage of growth is reached when one becomes a *teknion* referring to the turbulent teen years between adulthood and childhood.[23] That is the time when one exhibits both characteristics often in unequal proportions. Usually just enough to give a parent hope maybe they will grow up after all.

It is a time when parent gives more and more responsibility and trust to this child man to merit further trust. The *teknion* stage is perhaps the longest period of development because the child is reaching for the prize of maturity which is the final destination growing.

In the Jewish economy, full growth into manhood was not reached until age 30. So the young adulthood was distinguished as a *Huios* (pronounced whee-os) no longer a child but a son who can accept greater responsibilities and receives greater trust.[24]

When this stage is completed, a special ceremony is instituted called the *Huiothesia* spoken of in *Romans 8:15* as the *spirit of adoption*, and in *Galatians 4:4-5*, "But, when the fullness of time was come, God sent forth His Son, made of a woman, made under the law, to redeem them that were under the law, that we might receive the adoption of sons."[25]

Literally, *huiothesia* means the placing as sons with full sonship rights. We have received the Holy Spirit as a producer of relationship with the Father as son to Father, no longer a child.

It is the picture of the prodigal son returning from his years of wasting his substance to receive the signet ring of full authority to act in place of his father to buy and sell.

In other words, he received his father's power of attorney. You do not give this power to just anyone; it is only given to those who have proven their right to be trusted. Jesus received the total trust of the Father when the Holy Spirit descended on him in the form of a dove and a voice spoke from heaven saying "This is my beloved son in whom I am well pleased. Hear ye him."

When you can be trusted to exercise the gifts properly, God will take you beyond the care of mentors and tutors to be and act on your own. He will be able to say, you know my will well enough to go forth without the constraints of servant hood and can now act as sons of authority. Child you have grown up.

As side comments, let me say the greatest errors and blunders of the Church has been to release children to do the work and ministry of adult sons. Preachers, teachers and prophets alike jumped into their ministries as soon as they were called but before they were placed.

Note, Barnabas and Paul did not go on their called missionary journey until they were confirmed and commissioned by the Church leadership. An immature ministry has so much ability to be destructive that it must be thoroughly trained and equipped before unleashing them to minister.

Putting a Face on Doctrine

I remember well the night I received Jesus Christ as my Lord and Savior on November 12, 1944 as a lad of 15. A dear Brother in the church, a man I saw as old, came to me and gave me the best advice I could have received then. "Charles you don't know how to pray or what to pray for. First pray for wisdom. Second, study the first nine chapters of Proverbs they are the advice of a father. (King David to his son Solomon) Third, if you will pray and read your Bible, the two of them together fifteen minutes a day you will never backslide."

While I did not always keep that schedule, I did pray enough and read my Bible enough to maintain my spiritual life up to this present time. Immediately, I began a reading regimen that took me through the Bible in my first year as a Christian. The thirst for reading the Word propelled me as a young evangelist to dig deeply for I recognized my ignorance of the Word could not be tolerated if I were to preach truth. You cannot preach, teach or effectively live truths you do not know.

As a young preacher I went into used bookstores, Salvation Army stores, Goodwill stores where I could afford to buy books cheaply. Doing this, I learned to discriminate between good books and bad ones. Not everyone who writes or preaches about the Bible believes the Bible is the Word of God.

The Word I placed in my heart became my safeguard against wrong doctrine. Study became a pattern of life for me. It built up strongholds in my spirit against error. This bulwark has enabled me to correct aberrant behavior in myself and others; the truth always brings freedom.

As the Word of God became my compass and my guide, it set the parameters for any revelation received, not my mystical experiences. Everything must stand before the acid test of, "What does the Word of God say?"

Chapter Notes:
1. Acts 15-43.
2. I Timothy 5:1.
3. Parakaleo - mean to sit down with, near to, to call alongside, to invite, to entreat, to pray for, and to cover alongside. W.E. Vines, *Expository Dictionary of New Testament Words.*
4. Acts 2:40.
5. Crooked meaning to bend out of shape. W.E. Vines, *Expository Dictionary of New Testament Words.*

6. Acts 27.
7. Acts 27:23.
8. Titus 2,3.
9. I Timothy 4:13.
10. I Timothy 4:12.
11. 2 Corinthians 13:8-13.
12. *Nepios* refers to a nonspeaking child in other words a child who cannot yet communicate in proper language. *W.E. Vines, Expository Dictionary of New Testament Words.*
13. I Corinthians 3:1.
14. *Nephos* is always associated with immaturity or the failure to develop to adulthood. *W.E. Vines, Expository Dictionary of New Testament Words.*
15. A man *aner* as distinct from a child but not just an *antropos* meaning a member of the human race, rather a distinct person among many men. *W.E. Vines, Expository Dictionary of New Testament Words.*
16. *Brephos* meaning an unborn child (a fetus) or a newborn infant. *W.E. Vines, Expository Dictionary of New Testament Words.*
17. Luke 1:41.
18. Luke 2:12.
19. 2 Timothy 3:15.
20. I Peter 2:1-5.
21. *Paidion* is used to describe the development of a *nepios* one totally under the care and training of its mother to the hands of its father. *W.E. Vines, Expository Dictionary of New Testament Words.*
22. I Corinthian 14:18-20
23. *Teknion* referring to the turbulent teen years between adulthood and childhood. *W.E. Vines, Expository Dictionary of New Testament Words.*
24. *Huios* (pronounced whee-os) no longer a child but a son who can accept greater responsibilities and receives greater trust. *W.E. Vines, Expository Dictionary of New Testament Words.*
25. *Huiothesia* means the placing as sons with full sonship rights. *W.E. Vines, Expository Dictionary of New Testament Words.*

CHAPTER 11

SPEAKING PROPHECY WITH COMFORT

Blessed be the Father of our Lord Jesus Christ, the Father of all mercies, and the God of all comfort. Who comforts us in all our tribulations, that we may be able to comfort them who are in trouble, by the comfort with which we ourselves are comforted. —2 Corinthians 1:3-5

CB

Prophecy Notes:

☐ Nothing Separates Us From the Love of God

☐ The Answer to Troubling Situations Is Always Cheer Up

☐ The Comfort of Hope

☐ Dangers of Mixing Legalism & Grace

☐ New Testament Prophecy & the Role of Admonishment

☐ Putting a Face on Doctrine

Comfort has become limited in its range in modern day thinking especially by men who don't consider it. Mainly women on the other hand are conditioned by their roles as mothers as nurturers to give comfort. Others know instinctively the power of comfort they open their arms and their hearts to their crying child. It is to the mother the hurt one usually runs to for comfort with both hurt feelings and skinned knees. She can apply the bandages of soothing words as well as medicine. Fears and tears are wiped away with her mercy.

Spiritual comfort covers with a broad blanket pains of rejection, denial, abandonment and the sins of a blighted past. Comfort picks up the fallen one with words of renewed trust and faith. "Let me help you up, Brother; I believe your future is still bright. God still loves you.

Such was the attitude of Barnabas toward John Mark, even though it meant leaving the Apostle Paul. He took Mark under his wing and believed in him. John Mark wrote the Gospel of Mark. All too often the Church has abandoned its wounded to repair themselves when a comforting word would have meant so much and helped bring restoration.

The Apostle Paul wrote to the Church in *1 Thessalonians* not only to correct their misconceptions concerning the return of Jesus Christ.[1] They feared that those believers who died before the Return of Jesus would never see the Return. Paul comforted them with the words, "...the dead in Christ shall rise first and so shall we ever be with the Lord. Wherefore comfort you one another with these words." *Maranatha* meaning, "Behold the Lord cometh!"

Nothing Separates Us from the Love of God

I am reminded of a story I once read of a widow with several children to feed and educate. She did so by long years of drudgery taking in washings without modern conveniences. After her children were grown they decided to take mother on a trip from the known world in a four-room cottage in a Midwestern small town. They took her to see the ocean.

As she stood on the shores of the great Atlantic, she began to weep. When her troubled children asked why? She replied: "It's the first time I've ever seen enough of something!" These were the emotions expressed by the Apostle Paul in *Romans 8: 38-39*, "For I am persuaded that neither death, nor life, nor angels, nor principalities, nor powers, nor things present, nor things to come, nor height, nor depth, nor any other creature, shall be able to separate us from the love of God, which is in Christ Jesus our Lord."[2]

The love of God is beyond measuring, it is comprehensive, the all-encompassing love of God. With our limited capacities of understanding we can only marvel and wonder at such a display of pure grace. This *agape* love surpasses everything that passes for love in modern man's vocabulary. *Eros* is the physical love of testosterone gone wild.

Most people don't know the difference between aroused passions and deep love. Passion dissipates with the light of the next morning. The flames kindled by passions are not enough to maintain a marriage or a relationship. They last only until the next vision of loveliness appears or the next knight in shining armor arrives on the scene.

God's love is not engendered by passing attitudes or renewed promises of faithfulness. God's love precedes out of His nature not ours. We who have tasted the sweetness of the kisses of divine grace have received the mighty gift and its power to transform.

The indescribable heights to which we climbed were beyond our ability to achieve on our own. Every evil condition of our lives fell before the reach and power of His grace to love without limits. Those impossible walls of the Jericho that surrounded our destiny must fall before love's onslaught.

I am more than a conqueror through Christ who strengthens me is more than a hope; it is a fact of the lifting power of love. The trust in that love carries us to our destiny.

The Answer to Troubling Situations Is Always Cheer Up

There are several Greek words that are translated **comfort** or *Eupacheo* meaning be in good spirits, feel encouraged, cheer up, also *Tharseo* meaning cheer and comfort.[3] This is the comfort spoken of in *Philippians 2:19*, "But I trust in the Lord Jesus to send Timothy shortly to you, that I may be of good comfort, when

I know of your state."[4]

Sometimes comfort, good spirits, encouraging feelings are the result of a person, despite circumstances. I said earlier, that he (Apostle Paul) knew that Timothy would send a good report because Timothy looked on the bright side of things. He always saw things from a proper spiritual perspective; he was an encourager.

In *Matthew 9:2*, To a paralytic on a bed that was lowered through a hole in the roof, Jesus said, "...be of good cheer (be comforted) thy sins be forgiven thee."[5] What did his sins have to do with his paralysis? It had everything to do with it. When he was released by forgiveness of sins, his paralysis was healed instantly. Jesus had to go into a theological discussion to establish that healing and forgiveness are part of the same package.

Why would any sane man argue with the results? Yet the religious mind always does. When confronted with healing testimonies the religious relegate them to psychosomatic disorders that have no real basis in the physical other than a reaction to emotional attitudes.

Or a doctor may declare the disease is in remission as a natural explanation for a miracle. Despite all the natural exclamations, the evidence confronts us. The healed paralytic takes up his bed and walks. In verse 22 we have the account of the woman with the issue of blood who touched the hem of the garment of Jesus.[6]

What is not apparent to the western mind is that when she touched Jesus she made Him ceremonially unclean and made her subject to severe punishment. No wonder she came in the press of the crowd. Who knows how many other men she touched and made unclean? The prospect of revelation would have exposed too much anger and judgment, perhaps even to the point of being stoned to death. Jesus said "...Daughter, be of good courage; your faith has made you whole." Be comforted, no judgment is impending, only grace.

What would be your attitude if you were in a boat and facing a storm when a man comes walking on the water? What would be your response to such a sight in the middle of a crisis situation? Probably, you would think you were seeing a ghost or at least hallucinating.

Matthew 14:27 tells how Jesus meets the situation: "...He spoke to them saying, be of good cheer (be comforted), it is I, be not afraid."[7] The answer to troubling situations is always "cheer up," for cheering up always precedes deliverance.

Right when the whole boat load thought they were collectively losing their minds, faith is borne in the process of cheering up. Isn't it strange that no one today is desired outcome of our faith? It is not hard to be patient when you KNOW THE RESULTS AHEAD OF TIME. Faith knows, not hopes. Patience under girds faith until faith becomes sight.

Prophecy Note: The Comfort of Hope

There is a sound rustling in the leaves as a gentle breeze awakening, sending the thrill of life's movement. Ah, the refreshing wind that quickens, enriches, and fills the lungs with invigorating power. Hear the words that bring resurrection life to dead hopes and aborted dreams.

Such dreams that lie buried in the tombs of failures and defeats of the forgotten past. The winds of the Spirit declare that this is the season for the reawakening of the forgotten past they have been dammed up the lakes of pains from failure and rejection.

The dream once given is never forsaken in the mind and intent of the Father's determinate will. This is not the voices of stagnate minds that refuse to move from the dead past. It is the voice that declares and reaffirms the dream of yesterday. That dream though unfulfilled still has life for tomorrow.

The destiny designed in the heart of the Father is yet the same plan and direction for you. Walk toward the face of the future with reverence and expectancy for the step you take will open the pathway for succeeding generations. There is no defeat for faith, only victory and expanding opportunities. Take the venture to be a pacesetter, a pioneer for others to follow.

Dangers of Mixing Legalism with Grace

2 Corinthians 1:3-5 states, "Blessed be the Father of our Lord Jesus Christ, the Father of all mercies, and the God of all comfort. Who comforts us in all our tribulations, that we may be able to comfort them who are in trouble, by the comfort with which we ourselves are comforted."[8]

For as the sufferings of Jesus Christ abound in us; so our consolation also abounds by Christ." Our **tribulation** from the Greek word *thillibo* means affliction, to be under pressure, as the result of pressure from circumstances, or antagonism of people.[9]

The Apostle himself was under incredible pressures. Jewish Christians who were tied to their Old Testament doctrines followed him everywhere he went trying to subvert the gospel of grace by combining grace with law. These were astounded that Jesus walked on water but were appalled when Peter tried to?

Yes, but Jesus was different from Peter. Apparently not, or Jesus would have told him so. Peter you are only a man, I'm the Son of God. That was not the way Jesus reacted, "Come" is what he said. In comfort Jesus became their *Paraclete*, the full meaning of which is to call to one's side, console, encourage with the ability to give aid – our legal assistant, advocate, and an intercessor. Take note, all of these ministries are positive in action and results.[10]

Romans 15:4-5 "For whatsoever things were written in early times were written for our learning, that we, through patience and comfort of the scripture, might have hope. Now the God of patience and consolation grant you to be like minded (patient and consoling) one to another according to Christ Jesus."[11] Twice in these verses patience is urged by our advocate.

This character is so much more than passivity. Passivity may be nothing more than surrender to life's circumstances. Patience is waiting under fire with full confidence in the day. Legalism tries to bring the Church under bondage of the law, reducing grace to being dependent on works. Works are then the work of human effort, rather than the finished work of Jesus Christ.

They put the cart before the horse. Making our salvation depend on what we do rather than making works proceed from salvation. How many are the victims of hopes lost and dreams of righteousness destroyed by legalism. Robbed of grace, they find dependence on the works of the flesh is a broken crutch because works are never good enough to merit God's favor.

The desperation of never being able to climb the ladder of holiness ends in frustration, hopelessness, and dejection. Add to this doctrinal problem, the Apostle had the care of the Churches. Paul had to preach the elemental doctrines of righteousness to the Romans.

The Galatians' churches were so quickly turned aside from grace to legalism Paul wondered who bewitched them? The Corinthian Church was a mish mash of amazing gifts coupled with terrible disorder. The church was lacking in the grace of love and needed reassurance the resurrection had taken place. The Church at Thessalonica was torn with conflicting opinion about the Lords return.

The Church at Colosse was under attack with weird doctrines that placed angels above Jesus Christ as the Gnostics proclaimed that they had superior knowledge. In his personal letters to Timothy, Philemon and Titus he carried the load of Apostleship as their mentor. As if that were not enough he gives the horrendous list of physical tortures and privation in *2 Corinthians chapter six, verses one through ten.* [12]

But wait a minute; to all this pressure let us add the last straw, a thorn in the flesh. The thorn in the flesh brought urgent pleadings for its removal, to no avail. Wow, talk about having your plate full.

Yet here he is comforting others, becoming their advocate, their assistance and aid. Most of us would be in a fetal position of self-centeredness crying out "Somebody help me!" So, I conclude that no matter how difficult we are always expected to be ready to give comfort to the needy around us.

New Testament Prophecy & the Role of Admonishment

The word *admonish* is added because so many desire to use this word as their excuse to give negative and judgmental prophecies. They use this word to define **exhortation**. The word admonish and its included verbs and adverbs are translated from two basic Greek words: the *Nauthesia* meaning the mind to put, in other words to put an idea in the mind.[13]

The meaning is to put an idea of reasonability in the mind. In the process of teaching, edifying, exhorting, and comforting ideas are placed in the mind that will govern behavior. Listen to the words of wisdom from the Apostle Paul to the Church of Ephesus in *Ephesians 6:4*, "And you fathers provoke not your children to wrath, but bring them up in the nurture and admonition of the Lord."[14]

Nurture means *Paideuo* or training, chastening which can also mean correcting by demanding correction, not necessarily beating or harshness.[15] In other words let Jesus be our example in correcting and disciplining, not only of our children, but of one another.

Jesus spent three years in training His disciples without one instance where in harshness he rebuked them, chastised them or in any way demeaned them. Even His rebuke was gentle. In *Luke 22:31-32* Jesus spoke to Peter: "Simon, Simon, behold, Satan has desired to sift you as wheat; but I have prayed for you, that your faith fail not and when you are converted, strengthen the brethren."[16]

The method of sifting wheat in Bible times was to beat the grain with a flail till the grain was loosened then to throw the whole bundle into the air so the wheat would fall to the ground while the chaff would blow away. The devil wishes to beat us and thrash us, not Jesus. He believed in His prayers for Peter. He did not remove the temptation from Peter; rather He prayed that his faith fail not. Can you trust your prayers of intercession? If not, why not?

2 Thessalonians 3:11-15, "For we hear that there are some who walk disorderly; working not at all but are busybodies. Now them that are such we command and exhort, by our Lord Jesus Christ, that with quietness they work and eat their own bread but you brethren, be not weary in well doing. And if any man obeys not our word by this epistle; note that man and have no company with him, that he may be ashamed. Yet count him not as an enemy but admonish him as a brother."[17]

Disorderly was a military term which meant to break ranks, to be out of step.[18] Whether they are overly excited and are getting ahead of the Lord or officious meaning offering their services where they are not needed or wanted. Or if they are just plain lazy (always lagging behind), the problem must be addressed by admonishment.

Put words in their minds, words that will point them in the right direction. The idleness led them to become busybodies. It was a practice of the magicians of that day to be taken up with trifles, a pattern followed by these busybodies, magnifying small things as major problems.

How many pulpits major in minors in the guise of concern about verities? Paul left the Church with directive in dealing with such people, cut them off from fellowship. Do not allow them to disrupt the fellowship of the church; they are not living by faith but by mooching off others and are walking in disobedience to the Word of God.

Don't treat them as enemies but as brothers admonish them. Admonish them how? Reminder of the words that are to work in quietness (keeping their mouths shut) and eat their own bread.

Titus 3:8-11 puts it like this, "This is a faithful saying, and these things I will that you affirm constantly, that they who have believed in God might be careful to maintain good works. These things are profitable unto men, but avoid foolish questions, and geologies, and contentions, and strivings about law; for they are unprofitable and vain."[19]

A man is considered a **heretic** when he dissents from an accepted belief or doctrine. (The Greek word *hairetikos* means capable of choosing, a self-willed opinion which is often substituted for submission to the power of truth, that leads to division and formation of sects causing a party spirit and factions.)[20] After the first and second admonition, reject this person, knowing that he that is subverted *ekstrepho* meaning to turn inside out, to change entirely and sins, being condemned of himself."[21]

Paul warns of foolish questions (foolish meaning *moros* to scorn the heart and character), foolish describes a morally corrupt man.[22] This man admonish twice then reject. Make a clean-cut of fellowship. Notice the path the heretic follows: foolish questions, genealogies and contentions (*Eris* meaning strife and debate.)[23]

Being a heretic is much more than being in error, it is a conscious choice of one to believe their own word and ideas over the Word of God. These people are irredeemable; these are the same people that God turns over to a reprobate mind to believe a lie. The Hold Spirit always brings unity.

Perhaps I have belabored the point, yet I make no apology.

The ministry of prophecy in the church is consistent, never varying in its purpose. The mission of the Holy Spirit is to gather the church; it is to bless the church to grow to the fullness of the Body of Jesus Christ. To be boldly frank with you, if you are not making the effort with your prophecy to under gird with love, then keep silent, you will do more harm than good. You have been chosen as a conduit for the mind and heart of Jesus Christ; do not allow that word to be tainted or flawed by self-will or self-delusion. Bless the people of God with a pure motive. Follow the New Testament pattern of prophecy in 1 Corinthians 14:3.[24]

Putting a Face on Doctrine

Were it not for the fact that I know when I have heard the voice of God, it would be the height of arrogance to attempt to prophesy to anyone. However, the urgency of the message heard in the now about the future of someone's future constrains me to give them the message heard in my spirit.

In all cases, I have nothing to gain personally by prophesying to another except the satisfaction of obedience to God and a clear conscience toward man. I may or may not be received. Has that ever happened to me? Resoundingly yes! There have been those who made my revelation a joking matter.

Others refused to receive the message; because it conflicted with their agenda or they had other priorities for their lives. Does that dissuade me? No, my objective is to deliver the message not to force them to any action. My constant effort is to bless people; I don't try to make people receive such help gladly.

All may prophesy and all do, most with out knowing it. They may relate to a friend or prayer partner a feeling, a sense that God is moving in a certain direction, or urging them in someway. That is prophecy; it's just prophecy in an unthreatening manner. I am comfortable with my friend where I might be very uncomfortable with mere acquaintances or strangers.

Chapter Notes:

1. I Thessalonians.
2. Romans 8:38-39.
3. *Eupacheo* meaning be in good spirits, feel encouraged, cheer up, also *Tharseo* meaning cheer and comfort. W.E. Vines, *Expository Dictionary of New Testament Words.*
4. Phillipians 2:19.
5. Matthew 9:2.
6. Matthew 9:22.

7. Matthew 14:27.
8. 2 Corinthians 1:3-5.
9. *thillibo* means affliction, to be under pressure, as the result of pressure from circumstances, or antagonism of people. *W.E. Vines, Expository Dictionary of New Testament Words.*
10. *Paraclete Paraclete*, the full meaning of which is to call to one's side, console, encourage with the ability to give aid – our legal assistant, advocate, and an intercessor. *W.E. Vines, Expository Dictionary of New Testament Words.*
11. Romans 15:4-5.
12. 2 Corinthians 6:1-10.
13. Nauthesia *Nauthesia* meaning the mind to put, in other words to put an idea in the mind. *W.E. Vines, Expository Dictionary of New Testament Words.*
14. Ephesians 6:4.
15. Paidoue *Paideuo* or training, chastening which can also mean correcting by demanding correction, not necessarily beating or harshness. *W.E. Vines, Expository Dictionary of New Testament Words.*
16. Luke 22:31-36.
17. 2 Thessalonians 3:11-15.
18. Disorderly was a military term which meant to break ranks, to be out of step.
19. Titus 3:8-11.
20. *Hairetikos* which means capable of choosing, a self-willed opinion which is often substituted for submission to the power of truth, that leads to division and formation of sects causing a party spirit and factions. *W.E. Vines, Expository Dictionary of New Testament Words.*
21. *Ekstrepho* meaning to turn inside out, to change entirely and sins, being condemned of himself. *W.E. Vines, Expository Dictionary of New Testament Words.*
22. *Moros* to scorn the heart and character), foolish describes a morally corrupt man. *W.E. Vines, Expository Dictionary of New Testament Words.*
23. *Eris* meaning strife and debate. *W.E. Vines, Expository Dictionary of New Testament Words.*
24. 1 Corinthian 14:3.

CHAPTER 12

THE POWER OF PROPHETIC VISION AND SONG

There is only one Church, one Body….There is no Church within the Church that has greater favor with God. —*Charles Rosson*

ย

Prophecy Notes:

☐ The Seeing Eye of a Prophet

☐ Lord Anoint My Eyes to See

☐ What the Spirit Sees

☐ Power of Prophetic Song

☐ Songs My Spirit Hears

☐ New Songs of the Spirit

☐ It Was Him

Sweet are the meditations of the prophets for he or she is invited into the throne room of the Father to hear the beating of His heart and the agenda of His purpose. What treasure unfolds as the intentions of God are revealed with personal direction to achieve those goals.

The prophet gets to laugh at the feeble efforts of Satan to prevent the divine purposes of the Father. As the days of culmination are being reached the immutable march of righteousness continues.

For the Dallas Metropolis there is coming a mighty influx of spiritual growth and power. The upsurge of spiritual presence and influence will alarm the media for they will seek answers for this apparent phenomenal explosion.

As they seek answers in the natural world they will concoct all sorts of foolish responses such as: an emotional backlash for supposed evils of our age, a reaction to the left wing liberal shifts as seen on both the East coast and West coast intelligentsia. The media will have a hard time identifying the real reason. It is not a going back to old paths in reactionary responses but a leaping forward into a higher realm of moral responsibility to the society around us.

Cutting edge Christianity is far more than conservatism returning to outmoded mores of puritan days of yesteryear; it is springing from the foundations of everlasting truths to new perspectives for modern man. These new perspectives will catapult the Church into 21st century methods of facing the basic problems of life today with answers to critical questions that confront each of us.

The complexities of modern life are still nothing more than questions that have faced men since times beginning. "Who am I? Where am I going? What is the meaning of life?" These questions may be dressed in more modern garments but the real issues of man are as basic as ever.

Where does the prophet fit in this picture? He stands alongside the Apostle exploring the avenues of the new. He sees new answers for old problems. He sees past the masks of false identities that plague men who become actors following the scripts written by others. They make-believe a confidence unrealized by the real self. They play on a stage a joyous happy self that has to rely on drugs (prescribed and otherwise) to make it from one day to the next.

They are anesthetized by the constant barrage of sports, sex, entertainment etc. till the façade has become the building itself and the real is submerged into oblivion. The art of being a genuine person is becoming lost by so many in our world today.

The modern age is consumed with appearances, cosmetology (not just improving appearance) demonstrates the utter hatred of the real person that was. All this is done to try to receive the friendship and acclaim that is absent in the inner self. The prophet can show the way to a new celebration.

A celebration of who I am! A noteworthy person made so uniquely and distinctively that I have been chosen to impact the world around me. MY world, regardless of its size is my world. It may or may not impress others, but it is my sphere of action and authority.

The Seeing Eye of the Prophet

As the shutter size and speed of a camera determine the light the camera receives, in the same way my soul decides the amount of truth I can digest at one time. The more my conscious mind (pusche the soul) is filled with the Word of God the more truth is available to my spirit to build on.

I speak the desire of my heart when I say: "Lord, take in the fuller revelation of your truth that my world may understand and receive the wonders of grace you have reserved for it. Enlarge my paradigm so I see the inclusion of the entire family of God with its many ranges of color, customs and ethnology with unprejudiced eyes of acceptance and love."

I must not become abusive, reclusive or exclusive for I shall become an unused unneeded appendage in the Body of Christ. There is only one Church, one Body.... There is no Church within the Church that has greater favor with God. "Let me not become obsessed with familiar faces, familiar conditions and familiar doctrines.

Condition my spirit to accept all truth but only truth. Please direct me to revealed truth, both new and expanded; else I will stagnate in the morass of past errors and confusion. Holy Spirit, you are my assigned teacher, dilate my lens of spiritual receivership to its fullest capacity at this moment. Tomorrow I shall seek more!"

As the camera seeks new images to project as living, vibrant pictures, so seeks my spirit to bring to life the images planted in my spirit by the Holy Spirit. Contained in those pictures are images of the past that give new understanding of my present and future. In the now, I can see my place in God's understanding of life.

Thankfully, there are also portraits of the future taken from God's gallery of potential for me. So I open my spiritual shutters to receive my hopes and dreams of destiny. What I have seen I can achieve! Even more I will achieve!

What have you seen? Abraham, who lived life on the move, saw an enduring city eternal in the heavens. What wonderful audacity has the dreamer who believes in the pictures from his spirit.

Lord Anoint My Eyes to See

Lord anoint our eyes with eye salve to heal our blindness. Far too long the Church world has suffered from the blurred vision of astigmatism. With astigmatism inducing little or no vision for proper direction of God's people, they have relied on denominational direction from hierarchy centuries dead. The traditions of yesterday may have only limited application to the circumstance of today. (I am not referring to principals and laws of Divine truth, these are inviolate and immutable.)

The foundational truths are more than the changing opinion of men or the distorted alterations of the *Logos* Word of God. Many in the "Church" are led by those in leadership who are near sighted and can see nothing beyond their little circle and their ivory towers of isolationism. Their whole program is self-centered, self-righteous and self-serving.

Others are so visionary and idealistic that they cannot serve in a practical way the needs of humanity. They are beyond being visionary and are become mystics hidden in the caves with those who have lost relativity to the present. Blissfully they sail for distant shores while failing to see the challenges of the present.

There are those with tunnel vision who have such limited focus that they never can see the "Big" picture. They require a telescope or a microscope for they see only the microdot immediately before them. Hidden from them are enemies or opportunities on either side of them.

So again, I ask anoint our eyes to see the events of today as you see them. Open our eyes to the world around us with your perspective. Dear Father, help us to see beyond the filth of sin fallen brothers and sisters who need our love, understanding and support. Give us eyesight to look beyond race, color or creed with eyes of love and healing. I can never bring the life of God to others until *agape*, the God quality of love matures in me.

What the Spirit Sees

Who can adequately describe the scenes beheld by the eye of the spirit? Who can see the glories of future hopes and the destinies of the newborn believers? This dream has been imprinted and implanted into their spirit man. This divine etching on the subconscious inner man, this mystery of heavenly purpose is not to hide from but to hide for them in the inner kingdom to protect the vision from dream thieves.

The revelation will come as intimate relationship with the Father is developed. The fullness of the mystery of divine purpose may come in one fell swoop but more often in bits and pieces as we are able to process them and act on the knowledge received. The Apostle Paul was one of the few to whom God could give full revelation to in a onetime vision of his future. He saw not only glories of distant dreams but also the pains to be endured to complete his mission successfully.

The revelation of the future which God sees in the continuous "now" creates such unspeakable joy and anticipation that we are lifted in those moments above our present circumstances. The hopes seen by the eye of faith are of such inspiration that they quicken the spirit, soul and body to act as a unit toward the unseen goal.

Never am I more integrated than at that moment! It is at this moment that ignorance is exchanged for knowledge, poverty for abundance, power for impotence. From the acorn of small things springs the mighty oak that will last for centuries. Do not allow the pessimism of those who do not dream to deter you in your pursuit of destiny.

Your dream and its largeness determine your destiny. Then you too will declare: "For this cause was I born, for this reason came I into the world."

The Power of Prophetic Song

The song is freedom's release coming forth in clamorous praise. The tears on cheeks inflamed with joy, poured in torrents which once had known only pain and despair.

The song of sin's chains broken unleashes torrents unabated pleasures. A new man arose from the death of the old. The song of new life echoes from shore to shore crossing over the oceans that once proclaimed death and defeat.

The song of new vision and new purpose left the numbing cold of old plans now dead and buried in a forgotten past. Life is now seen from the lofty heights of God's perspective. The song of faith has determined possibilities and opened new horizons of hopes brightest dreams.

The song awakens from the death of the past, anew creation of God's everlasting purpose. The song reveals the beauty, the power, and the treasures known in the heart of God. For He knew from eternities past; he knew the seed to plant inside you the view that surpasses even heavens splendor.

The song opens the unseeing eyes to see the destiny of God's promised ones. The song penetrates the deaf ears of hardened hearts with dancing notes of high praise. The deaf ear that could only hear sounds in the head, can now hear externally as well, the sound of the music once locked inside the heart.

The song is sung especially in the nighttime and causes the night to glow as the noonday sun with God's revelation truth.

Songs My Spirit Hears

The first songs my spirit heard were the funeral dirges of hopes near dead. They were songs of incredible pain, where I saw dreams slowly dying of the starvation by lack of faith. My songs in those days of desolation were the groans of rejection long felt. Sadly, then no one sang my songs of sorrow leaving me alone in my distress. Thus my agony was prolonged by my isolation. No one heard my song!

Gradually the darkness was lifted as an early morning fog when the first rays of the sun began to burn away the pervasive gloom. Yet, there was a clinging to the known fears because the unknown cloak of suffering was too horrible to consider. Who would desire to enter an arena of further and greater rejection? Indeed worse possibilities were a constant threat of worse. Worse rejection, worse denial, worse! Just worse! It was through such attitudes the spirit heard a song of a different note. Faintly, a song of hidden dreams came from somewhere deep inside.

As the first rays of the sun crept over the horizons of my life, I heard the siren song of deep calling unto deep; urging me, nudging me to look up. Ah, the secret to solving life's problems with darkness are solved always by looking up! Even when the circumstances remain the same, look up! For our help is always from above. For too long, I allowed circumstances to dictate my attitude and emotions. Thus my ears could not hear the songs my spirit heard. The songs of hope and of joy awaited my willingness to hear.

Today a new song begins the upward turn of my life. Hope, joy, and peace break through the darkness to disperse the gloom that once covered me. I looked up! My spirit heard the announcement: "God never changes; His Word never fails!" Circumstances change when His voice speaks! Health in all forms is established when His voice speaks!

Worlds are altered at His Word; light shines, firmament divides itself. Life comes into being when He breathes. (What are words but breath over vocal cords, tongues, and lips to give distinction to that breath?) The process is unchanged through the centuries. God does everything according to the initial pattern.

The morning stars sang together in creation. So now songs of the spirit accompany the creations of the Father. The Spirit hovers over the void of our lives to separate the incompatible things of life to bring us to the place of seeing light. Light be and suddenly things unknown become clearly seen.

This is the song my spirit hears "Light Be!" For with light comes knowledge and understanding. The process continues until the Father looks with admiration and declares that all is good and very good. So begins the journey of grace to its ultimate goal, "Well done my good and faithful servant."

Such is the song my spirit sings, a song of the magnificent possibilities leaping on the stage of life's actualities. Achievements of grace and divine enabling elicit thunderous joy. Praise indescribable pours forth in torrents of never before felt worship. Emotions previously unknown and unexplored are now considered my "norm". Praise where were you hidden all these years? I have heard a new song in my spirit and the dungeons of darkness.

Released praise, riotous praise, roaring loud praise with shouts and whirling dances not choreographed by men. Worship no longer prostrate in silent adoration and no longer mute in awe; but loud vociferous worship that silences angels. Transcendent worship brings man to a new level of understanding our glorious God.

This worship will be heard by the world who cannot imitate its beauty, its power or its acceptance by the Father. The world will be shocked and amazed by the audacity of the songs my spirit hears.

The new songs of the spirit are designed to restore music in the Church to its paramount place as far superior the music the world has stolen to lure weak ones from the Father. There is an unprecedented drawing power to the music that my spirit hears to cross all cultural, racial and age boundaries. In deed men will hear the music of heaven on earth.

This song my spirit hears. Such majesty, such glory, such triumph, such victory! Finally men can see the multifaceted God with the reflected lights of millions of light rays that adorn His face. Eternity will never exhaust the continuous revelation of such brilliance.

New Songs of the Holy Spirit

New songs of the spirit are being heard from the heavens, songs of joy that make glad the earth. That joy is the expectations of all created beings eliciting hope's greatest promise. The blending of voices once divergent now congruent, from every ethnic background, from every age level, from every culture; now joined in spectacular praise of one Father and God of us all.

It is the music of hearts made free to marvelous joy, and redundant praise never before heard on earth's surface. Only the palace of heaven heard such melodies and echoed forth such magnificent praise. How pleased the Father must be! The languages of separation now unified as one voice with many layers of harmonic tonality.

The unity of joy will bring unity of expression as a symphony of unadulterated praise with no taint of competition or undue pride of voice. As praise opens the entry into the inner sanctum where worship occurs, there will be a mass of worshipers released to new songs, new melodies, new drumbeats accentuating the new songs.

You will hear the blending of music past, present, and future coming together in one majestic anthem new song. The upsurge of worship and praise will precede the mighty army God has gathered for the next movement of Divine purpose. This music will leap the walls of sectarianism, catapult the barriers of Islam, transcend the paradigms of mans misconceptions about the Father and bring in a new and deeper relationship between God and man.

The bastions of the enemy will crumble and fall flat as Jericho's walls as the might army of Judah's praise sends forth the music of the new song the Spirit has inspired. The foe can only cower behind the walls once thought impregnable and watch as God's people take back the land where the Saints have trod. The footprints of the past establish our right to claim and to conquer. Such songs of power, such songs of victory, such songs of triumph!

How do we come to hear such songs, songs that have been hidden from man till now? I ask are you willing to cut ties to yesterday's music. Are you willing to leapfrog from the present acceptability to tomorrow's new sounds? The songs of yesterday served their purpose but have become dated for today. The songs of today will not serve the age of tomorrow.

This is not to abandon yesterday and today but rather to meld them with the new. Mary, you have a special place in tomorrow's history as one who bridges the gap and joins the past and present with the future. Others will join you in the effort, but make no mistake; you are a pioneer in this majestic undertaking. As a pioneer you will have to be strong in the music you have heard. Let criticism roll off your back like water off a ducks back.

People always resist change. Nothing is as frightening as something new. Despite their initial fears they will be drawn irresistibly to the music that provides so much hope and joy.

Already you have heard disturbing tones of "How dare they shout from their lethargy where dreams have lost impetus and self-satisfaction abides. The new song will awaken the sleeping lion to go forth in search of the prey. The new song sets the cadence for the march of God's army. The new song both inspires and validates the struggles to come with prophecies of the victorious outcome.

The new song ushers in a new depth of worship where "knowing God" surpasses "knowing about God." Thousands on thousands will say "I have been in the secret place with my Father. I know my purpose and destiny because I have been with him." Since relationship always precedes purpose, we can understand why Jesus told the woman in Samaria the Father was seeking "Worshipers."

The key to all victory is knowing your purpose and following that path to destiny. All begins with worship. Praise is not for God but for warfare to discomfit the enemy and open the door to worship. Praise and worship have different goals and must never be used for their unintended purposes. Many are satisfied to praise but have never tasted the presence of the Father in the blackness of the solitude of the Holy of Holies.

This is not the solitude of loneliness but the privacy that rue intimacy demands. This is a private audience with my Father, where we can share our hearts without veiled face. "I know Him and He knows me." Here in the secret place is my dwelling of safety and security.

No enemy can intrude and no friend will. I can leave this presence with full assurance of His acceptance and protection that no evil shall come nigh my dwelling for I dwell in Him. Such fullness, such completeness, such wholeness and such holiness; all because of the moments I have spent with Him. And it all began with a new song.

It Was Him

It was more than a song, it was more than a prayer, and it was an awareness of Him. There was an awareness of Him. That awareness is both his majesty and His glory. That experience forever changed the landscape of life. The hunger shows that I have tasted of Him in such intimacy of sharing now demands constant feeding on Him and Him alone.

The acceptance and understanding received in that glorious moment, became the watermark for my daily worship. It was not in the singing, nor in the praying but in experiencing His presence. The melody of the song may fade in time. The subject of that initial prayer forgotten but the secret of His presence is ever fresh and always remembered.

How could I be accepted by Him when my past of sinfulness was established and proven beyond all question? The secret was in my being incarnate in His Son. Jesus the Son of God became God incarnate in the flesh. When I became a believer on Him as my Savior, I became man incarnate in His Godness.

Thus encapsulated in His righteousness I am accepted in the beloved and suddenly wholeness surrounded me like a blanket of security. No wonder the Psalmist in *Psalms 16:11* declared "In thy presence is fullness of joy." *Genesis 4: 16* the curse of Cain was enforced: "Cain went out from the presence of the Lord." No wonder Cain declared "My punishment is greater than I can bear." It was this thought that Jesus endured in Gethsemane that extracted great drops of blood in response.

The physical sufferings to be endured on *Golgotha* were horrendous indeed but separation from His Father even for three days was beyond His imagination. "Eli, Eli, elohim) sabach thani, My God my god why hast thou forsaken me?" was His last cry before He gave up his Spirit. What greater pain could be endured than that?

The scriptural declaration of the Apostle about our former life was that we were without God in this world. The presence of God changes everything, panoramas of hope blossom in the desert. New vistas of promise brighten the pathway of life with dreams long forgotten in the seas of failure.

It is in His presence that I reach the apex of all that I was designed to be. The surge of faith explodes with boldness to claim and proclaim thus the impossible not only becomes doable but an absolute fact. Dreams are more than fantasy and wishes. Dreams are the realities of tomorrow's hopes.

Everything begins with the dream and the dream begins in His presence. Through the eyes of faith the curtain of the future is pulled back for our anointed vision to see.

His presence makes solid ground for faith to walk into tomorrow. The unknown is explored by dreams and visions that create hope that activates faith. Hopes ignited by His presence mature into the results of faith's production. The grasp of faith is established by hope's vision. It all begins in His presence. In that august place of fellowship and intimate knowing of one another, the reborn one is thrust into the limitless expanse of possibilities and opportunities.

On the shores of the Sea of Galilee the Master called four men in rapid succession: "Follow me and I will make you fishers of men." Two thousand years have gone by and their message is still catching men. Peter and Andrew, James and John are yet casting their nets into the sea of humanity with ship sinking loads of men.

In His presence is your opportunity to touch, mold and shape the future. You are no longer a victim but an innovator, an activator to set in motion the plans of God in perpetuity. His presence is more than inspiration, more than motivation; it is life-giving, empowering, equipping, and releasing.

The Kingdom of God is unleashed for realization in His presence. Here love finds its greatest expression; joy flows as rivers of grace. Peace reigns in perfect manifestation. Such a King deserves our total obedience and worship.

CHAPTER 13

PROPHETIC DECLARATIONS

For whatsoever things were written in early times were written for our learning, that we, through patience and comfort of the scripture, might have hope. Now the God of patience and consolation grant you to be like minded (patient and consoling) one to another according to Christ Jesus. —*Romans 15:4-5*

ଔ

Prophecy Notes:

- ☐ Visions of Hope
- ☐ The Death of a Dream
- ☐ Breaking Forth
- ☐ Lead O King Eternal
- ☐ Freedom Quest
- ☐ The Wellsprings of the Holy Spirit
- ☐ The Winds of the Holy Spirit are Fanning the Flames

Everyone has a future and that future is limitless time. Our problem is that time is compartmentalized into past, present, and future. It is our understanding of time that places undue restrictions on us. We usually judge our futures on the basis of our past. If our past is the only indicator of our future then the quicker we quit life the better.

Yet men who broke the chains of the past are those who impacted our lives the most. Moses began his leadership of Israel at eighty years old, a ripe old age in any era. Abraham brought forth his progeny at one hundred years old. Joshua left his greatest legacy when he was one hundred ten years old.

Caleb at eighty five cries, "Give me the mountain where giants live; I need new enemies to conquer. The Anakims will be meat for the soup I will eat." He conquered Hebron and began the occupation that stopped war in that area of Judea.

These men counted their future as unlimited as eternity, because their names were written in eternities future hall of fame. There is no book of the dead in Heaven because God is not the God of the dead but of the living. We are always in the present with Him. No wonder the Word states nothing can separate us from the love of God in Christ Jesus. All things culminate in who God is and His divine purpose.

Set your sails for the long journey to dimly lit ports of call. There is a vast ocean to traverse. To reach the destination will bring you through many adverse winds and intemperate climates. Do not be dismayed at the problems but speak, "Peace be still," and the waters will become calm. Your safe arrival at heavens harbor is assured by His promises. Celebrate in the now for there is a final celebration to rejoice in later.

Visions of Hope

The tears in my eyes have distorted my vision with caricatures of hope, not the clear vision that is needed. My spirit groans to see the venues of hope with clarity. Deep inside me there is a place where dreams and visions reside. Jesus declared that "Kingdom of Heaven" was inside believing men and women. If heaven is inside, why do so many see only hell? It is because they do not unlock the Kingdom within.

Somehow, I know that beyond the slavery of ignorance, custom, and culture limitations there is an unchained me waiting to leap forth and shout: "Hello world, here I am!" So I wipe the tears of pain and frustration from my eyes so faith may rise to the level of my hopes and vision. The dream is so gorgeous that I must not lay dormant in my spirit. The world is waiting to see the beauty that I can produce.

How do I start the dream on its journey to fruition? Everything begins with a first step. Every parent remembers the first step of their child reaching into a whole new world of exploration. That first step was a monumental leap forward into the possibilities of life. For you, the first step is taking ownership of the vision God has given you.

Open your spirit to hear and accept in obedience the vision God has placed in you. You say the dream is too big for you, of course it is. God wants to pursue the adventure with you. It is on that journey that you will find God expanding your gifts exponentially.

After ownership what? It is time to lay foundations for the dream castle you are building. How deep you lay the foundation and the material you use to construct will decide the size of the structure that can be safely placed on it. So immerse yourself in the Word of God.

The baptism of the Word will erect a faith that cannot be shaken when troubled times come. There may be times when you have to remind yourself and God: "Father you called me and appointed me to this ministry. I didn't do it myself. I have been obedient so the results are up to you. The success or failure is in your hands." An unshakable faith will result in spectacular results.

The Death of a Dream

I saw a dream die! How can I explain the horror and pain that was endured? The extinguishing the light produced by the flame, brought a flood of hopelessness that was unendurable. When the killing of a dream is public the humiliation and shame are pervasive, leaving a corpse to be viewed by all.

More often the dream dies in the hidden privacy of the heart; like the crib death of a child with no apparent reason for death. Somehow in the secret chambers of the spirit, the dream died of inattention and unbelief. Or a host of negatives that smothered the child dream before it could express itself in words or action. In that moment life lost its purpose and meaning. From that moment the leader became a follower of those with lesser dreams. Life then becomes compressed into a mold that others determine.

Compromise has perverted the dreams of millions; when receiving approval or acceptance becomes more valuable than following the dream a perversion results. When such events take place, purpose is dissolved and vision is lost. An indistinct dream is no dream at all! The Apostle Paul said, "This one thing I do." He refused to alter his dream of destiny. A God given dream allows no alternatives or compromise.

The dream died of impatience and lack of trust. "Hope deferred maketh sick the heart," says the Proverbs of Solomon. We have so little respect for first steps because the goal seems so distant. Many dreams die because they are not under girded by faith and trust needed to complete the journey. The Hebrew writer encourages with, "Cast not away your confidence, which hath great recompense of reward."

Abraham at 75 had to wait an additional 25 years to receive the promised child. Age has nothing to do with the fulfilling of the dream. The prophet Joel prophesied "Your old men shall have dreams and your young men shall have visions". The dreams of the aged provide a fertile ground for the young to have visions. This is the bedrock for revelation's process.

I saw a dream die under the onslaught of mean vicious words. The dream was battered; it became children of murdered dreams in a surrounding sea of despair. The tender young dream was buried in a forgotten cemetery without a tombstone to witness its passing. In that forgetting, generations past, present and future are bereft of the possibilities of the dreams promise.

The God given dream holds all the potential of eternity. Every promise of the Word of God is realized when the dream is activated to fruition. The seedpod of the dream can be planted anew. Resurrect those forgotten dreams for they still reside in the secret chambers of your heart!

The events of the latest day's tragedy came crashing into my present-day realities so rapidly that I staggered under the load they placed on my shoulders. They reminded me of Job's ordeal, a parade of witnesses who informed him of each new horror. How swift are the feet of those who bring bad news!

Yet in the midst of evil tidings, we are constantly made aware of God's faithfulness and care for us. Without that support we would have fainted long ago. Thank God for the abundant flashes of glory and mercy in the nighttime of our deepest struggles. They were the uncountable stars that gave light to penetrate the darkness with direction and purpose.

These are times of constant contrasts, light and darkness each a requirement to reveal the beauty of one and the ugliness of the other. A diamond is best viewed against the black background of velvet. Righteousness shines best against the background of evil. When viewed against a neutral color, it diminishes and fades the clarity of each.

We in our present society have blurred the lines of good and evil by politically correct neutrality that accepts with equal force the views of all. The Church has become lukewarm and is only fit for God's rejection. Am I calling for the rabble-rousing of bigotry? Absolutely not! I am calling righteous indignation to direct our forces against the spirit realm of demons and demonic forces.

If we don't win the battle there, we will always be fighting blindly and ineffectively. The public media has desensitized us with the morphine of exaggeration, and distortion, in such vast quantities that our computer banks are overloaded.

While these truths are evident, do not be overcome with pessimism for the Lord God has not been taken unaware. He has raised up a Church of power and significance. Allow Israel to boast of the beauties of Zion. Jesus the Lord Advocate General makes his boast of his glorious Church. This is his chosen means of delivering the whole to the feet of the Father.

Look, see the Church, the majestic instrument to execute the will of God on the earth. It will be human hands energized by the Holy Spirit that deliver the Kingdom into the gratitude of the Father. Just as man brought the reign of Satan into the world, so shall man deliver the world back into the dominion of God.

Note, I am not referring to political regimes of fleshly under taking. I am referring to spiritually exercising the authority God has invested in us as the visible Body of Jesus Christ. Here and now my voice can be heard in whispers but it can be used as the voice of a lion, the roar of which shakes the nations. We are fast approaching the time when the Lion of Judah will sing songs that cause the nations to tremble and fall prostrate before such majesty.

Satan has dared to awaken a David to slay his Goliath who seemed invincible to the armaments of his day but only a stone in a shepherds sling, was needed to destroy him. I have arrayed many Davids with many stones to bring down the Goliaths that oppose me.

So, awaken o mighty army from the lethargy of dormancy. Arise with powerful arms and throw out the money changers within you; then attack the enemies on your doorstep. You are those who strike fear in the heart of the enemy. Darkness can never prevail against the laser beams of light.

Such a Church stands as the greatest achievement of the work of the Holy Spirit; He is no less successful than the Son of God was in His mission. With grace as our watchword, let us march together in this glorious cause.

From the vantage point of today, I can clearly see the mistakes, failures and errors of yesterday. They stand as monuments and tombstones in the graveyard of blighted hopes. The dead possibilities and dormant plans of destiny are forgotten. However my successes rise amid the rubble. However small they may seem to others, they establish my dreams, realize my hidden potentials and solidify my purpose and destiny.

So from my present position, however tenuous or trivial it may seem to others is my sacred ground of life. I yield it to no man! For it is ceded to me by the Lord God almighty. This is my portion of life; I cherish it and revel in it. So I close another year without apology. Without shame I declare that while the events of the past have shaped me; I do not fail to say I have climbed higher than yesterday!

There are no questions about the past, because the moment lived has climbed out of obscurity and any imperfections are readily exposed in my history. The unchangeable peaks and valleys once lived remain etched in the experiences of memory forever.

The events of the past remain as immutable history yet the conditions that produced them are subject to my alteration so that I can in my present weave a tapestry of hope. Hope has a grandeur all of its own. Hope exceeding hope; hope against hope climbs the steepest, most sheer mountain peak of impossibility.

Not merely defying death but more often defying life. It reaches beyond present realities to create an unbelievable adventure for faith to explore. How could such limitations be exceeded? The audacity of faith is to attempt such wonderful exploits.

The rising of faith is the precursor of sacred intervention. It is the weaving of God's miraculous intervention. His *dunamis* power released both in and through man. It is that marvelous mystery that has enabled men long dead to speak with relevance to our day and beyond it. The then unknown Apostles set the standards for life and purpose.

Divine words yes but they were words spoken by men, else they could not have gained entrance into the world. In God's economy, eternity waited in holy pause for a man to activate divine truth. Even now hope's promise lies sleeping awaiting faiths quickening, empowering words and deeds to bring to life the promise of hope and faith.

What of the future now hidden in the murky clouds of tomorrow? Here in this arena of the five senses, men rely on their memories to prognosticate or diagnose the possibilities of tomorrow. However, the analysis of the greatest brains of our day give no firm assurance of the futures content.

The only part of man that can give a clear picture of the future is the reborn human spirit led by the Holy Spirit. The spirit transports itself into tomorrow as easily as the mind peruses the past and present.

Hope paints the picture and lays the plans for faith to build. So faith constructs the vision, infused by the Holy Spirit into the spirit of man. What is your future? Tell me your dream for it declares your possibilities. The greatest tragedy is not being unable to fulfill your dream; it is in having no dream at all.

Better to fulfill only part of your dream than to wander aimlessly with no purpose or direction in life. The Bible is filled with the stories of men who did not complete their dream but the part they did complete marked them as great. For example, David, and Moses; what is the reach of your dreams? What is the span of your faith? That is the reality of your future!

Breaking Forth

The stark power of a dream from the inner man or the spirit of man breaks the blackness of darkness. The chains of ignorance; the limitations of status, lack of education, racial discrimination, or other artificial boundaries are leaped over in an instant.

That marvelous leap of the spirit transforms difficulties into victories; it turns defeats into transcending possibilities. The opportunities of the dream are world shaping when activated by faith's effort.

The dream motivates a person to new and raised positions. The fences of containment are erased and bypassed as nonexistent when one embraces the dream. What should be? What could be?

Then, become what will be! The vast potential of the dream is life's most unexplored territory. The borders of the forbidden are the armored garrisons that attempt to prevent your entrance into the wonderful world of dreams come true.

Access to the invisible and the improbable is the province of the dream. The dream is the incubation chamber of creativity that takes giant steps into new realities of the future. Answers to questions in every area of life are in the understanding of the dream.

The difficulties of the dream occur when the dream becomes adulterated, or tainted. When fear and doubt have painted their picture, the dream becomes a caricature of its original self. History is replete with dreams that became impure and distorted from the original version.

The realm of the spirit is controlled by dreams awakened within. This invisible realm comes alive with voices of direction and visuals aids when we decide to act on the dream given. Kingdom knowledge and understanding increase the strength of our stumbling steps as we begin to walk in our dream.

The expansion of this new Kingdom is enlarged when faith results in action. The ripple effect takes place when we cast our stones on the surface of life. We are often unaware of the effect we are having on those around us and the generations to come. It is in the reaching that we reach beyond our ability to reach.

Lead O King Eternal!

The march of warriors in lockstep shakes the ground and produces fear in the hearts of enemies as they tremble and quake in terror. Who could this mighty foe be? For hundreds of years the armies of perversity have held sway, who would dare defy the power and right to rule?

These powerful entities had exchanged the normal for the abnormal and subnormal till men no longer distinguished between them. All efforts to contain the advance of this mortal enemy had met with defeat and failure leaving the righteous to whine and cower in defeat. The carcasses of the fallen were left for birds of prey to feed on. Yet the sound of marching feet the sound of a mighty army continues. Who could this enemy be?

It is the sound of thousands and tens of thousands and thousands of thousands not only marching but singing the fierce songs of battle tested and battle hardened veterans. These are those who rush to the conflict with joy. Their cry is "I was made for this day, Lead on oh King Eternal for victory is ours." The craven cowards of evil slink behind their battlements in abject fear, their trusted walls no longer a defense against their united foe.

The marching feet of this mighty army sets up a pattern of sonic response that fells walls of the entrenched enemy. The songs of prophetic purpose cause a quaking of ten on the Richter scale and it is the prophecy of total defeat for demonic forces. Who is this mighty army? Where did they come from? Where were they hidden?

These are they who were birthed in the womb of faith's intercession, some in decades and centuries past. In the caves of seclusion they trained; their weapons of warfare were welded in their hands by constant and consistent use. They were trained by the prophets and warriors of yesterday's battles.

They are no longer a weak simpering mass but a well equipped forced ready and eager for battle. These each know their marching orders, the plan of battle is well defined; so march they as one singing songs of triumph. Satan, the nightmare that has plagued since Calvary and Pentecost has arrived!

Freedom Quest

On distant battlefields some aged, some new, covered with the blood of the dead and the wounded—freedom was purchased. Freedom and its pursuit is never an easy commodity to be obtained. Once gotten, it is only retained by constant vigilance.

Freedom once found will brook no substitutes; nor will she swear allegiance to imitations. For the soul of everyone cries out, 'Life without freedom loses all meaning without the freedom to make choices, the freedom to act, the freedom to believe and the freedom to explore the limits of life."

Even so, coupled with freedom is responsibility; for freedom does not exist in a vacuum. Personal freedom does not unchain me while I enslave others. It does not extend its borders to others then my freedom is diminished by the same amount that others are denied.

Freedom simply put allows me to make mistakes for which I must accept responsibility. Good choices will enrich me and others as well. Freedom gives me legal rights and moral rights that exercised wisely will benefit me as well as others.

Freedom opens doors of opportunity to a thousand rooms of hope. Every great move of history has come at the request of freedoms. Freedom called and governments and the governed changed. Thus was forged the lengthening steps of progress.

The future of freedom is kept in the imaginations and potentials of every person existent in the world. To reach its fullest measure many will have to have added cultures and traditions.

The expansiveness of the human heart can only be measured by the large steps of courage that brought man from his primal state to the present. Have all of man's steps been good? No but thankfully, many have been upward.

Whether the question of freedom for all humanity will be achieved in our lifetime is not the question. Will we continue the quest for freedom with the same passion that our forefathers did? That is the question. For <u>freedom is the noblest goal for any man</u>.

Treasure whatever gifts of freedom you possess. The fields of freedom's conquest are enriched by the blood of patriots. Honor those who gave so much to advance freedom's call and freedom's purpose. Peace and tranquillity are the footprints of freedom.

The Wellsprings of the Holy Spirit

Out of the wellsprings of the Spirit bubbles forth a continuing flow of hopes, dreams, visions, and aspirations. The streamlets of mercy will not be stopped by ordinary circumstances. There are enemies who would fill the wells with contaminates such as: anger, hate, unforgiveness, envy, strife, fear and an endless list of negative destructive forces.

The enemy would creep in the nighttime of our trials to bring hopelessness and despair. So vigilance and relationship with the Father must be protected always, guarding the heart for out of it flow the issues of life.

All of my life is contained in three compartments: my past, my present, my future. My past is a compilation of decisions, thoughts, and acts that are carved in the tombstone of yesterday. My present is my testimony of my perceived reality. My future is etched in the dreams and visions of God's perception of my destiny.

My dream places me in the possibilities of God's ordained pleasure. The hopes, faith and purposes of God for each of us are so majestic the natural mind staggers at such grandeur. How is it possible to rise to such height? Yet history is replete in examples of men and women who rose to the level of their dreams.

The dream calls us from obscurity to prominence, from darkness to light. We are called to break the chains of ignorance and defeat. Ignorance flees when one becomes a passionate seeker of knowledge. Defeat falls before the determined will to fight and conquer at all costs. The refusal to accept the terms of defeat are essential to eventual success.

The Winds of the Holy Spirit Are Fanning the Flames!

The winds of the Spirit are fanning the embers of almost dead fires to revive the long neglected dreams; dreams that have faded from disuse, neglect and lack of faith and action. I hear the Spirit say: the dream though dormant is still alive.

Fan the flame, put new fuel on the fire. Moses lived to be 120 years old; his life can be broken down into three segments of 40 years each. The first forty years he was educated to be a Pharaoh but nurtured to be a Hebrew.

What a contrast. No wonder he was conflicted and tried to free his people with Egyptian means rather than Hebrew faith. The second forty years was spent tending to the sheep of Jethro and meditating on the teachings of Jocebed his mother.

The last forty years he picked up again the dream of delivering his people. It is not too late to pick up the dream again! He fanned the flames of nearly dead dream till it burned such intensity that he did the unthinkable and delivered a nation to freedom.

The kingdom you are called to destroy may seem equally imposing. You may be seeing chariots being pulled by mighty war horses. But the winds of the Spirit are blowing up a sandstorm to confuse and delay the enemy till you can cross the parted waters of the Red Sea.

With the high walls of water congealed as jelly, you are given an abundant entrance toward your destination. So taking not only your nation but also the plunder of Egypt as back wages for 400 years of servitude you can now finance a new nation for God's glory.

So stop looking at the errors and sins of the past. They are of no consequence for the tomorrow. For your tomorrow will far exceed your yesterdays.

Don't stumble at your vision of things to come; for they are opening your eyes of *hope* and *faith.* Hope is the blueprint of desired results; faith is the building substance to materialize the dream.

The wind of the Spirit is blowing and its inspiration has awakened in you a shout of joy for you have heard wonderful words and caught glorious glimpses of the future's promise. My hands rise to praise the God of my salvation.

My eyes open wide with wonder for my dreams set the parameters for my future. There are no fences to keep me from my destiny. God's life has filled me with both dainties and strong meats to produce a joyful maturity in me

CHAPTER 14

PROPHETIC POETRY

I have a passion for tomorrow that has nothing to do with my present age. I have a passion for tomorrow for it is constantly opening a new page.
—*Charles Rosson*

C03

Prophecy Notes:

- ☐ I Have a Passion for Tomorrow
- ☐ Taking the Kingdom Into the World
- ☐ Your Kingdom Again
- ☐ Songs of the Prophet
- ☐ Rays of Hope
- ☐ Follow the Star
- ☐ Goodness Lined Her Face
- ☐ Anthems Raise
- ☐ I Must Go On

I Have a Passion for Tomorrow

I have a passion for tomorrow that has nothing to do with my present age.
I have a passion for tomorrow for it is constantly opening a new page.

I have a passion for tomorrow for it makes the proper use of
yesterday.
I have a passion for tomorrow because it overcomes all fears of
today.

I have a passion for tomorrow as the night time approaches,
I have a passion for tomorrow as the sunrise of opportunities
yet unfulfilled encroaches.

I have a passion for tomorrow for so much of life is yet to be
lived.
I have a passion for tomorrow for there is so much more that I
have to give.

Taking the Kingdom Into the World

I went into the world today and I took the Kingdom with me.
For deep inside the King lives for all the world to see.
So love met the world face to face in me for tender words were
spoken.

The smile of joy was more than me; it was a reflection of Him,
the King inside.
For face to face with Him I met in joyous union, spirit to spirit,
heart to heart, He held my hand our unity complete.

Such is the mind of a Kingdom person, we hear melodies
and lyrics, unknown to others; music, that originates in the
whispers of angels, infused with incredible power.

So to you friend I now declare: Take the Kingdom with you
wherever you go. So that your words, deeds and actions of
mercy demonstrate the Kingdom of grace that has power to
change lives.

The Kingdom is LOVE, JOY, AND PEACE FROM THE SPIRIT
that now reigns within. The outshining of Him will make light,
the dark days of life and beckon them to come in.

Your Kingdom Again!

We are bringing His kingdom to the world, for his kingdom
lives in me!
We are bringing His kingdom to this world for the king reigns
in us to see!

Come eat of the fruit of his table, righteousness, joy and peace
which the Holy Ghost brings to be.
I am bringing His kingdom to this world as His will shows forth
in me.

Hear now the songs of His kingdom aligning the church in
battle array
We are retaking the world from Satan, which he has led astray.

So we sing, Your Kingdom again! Your Kingdom again, Jesus
its your kingdom again.

The Songs of the Prophet

The songs of the prophet now heard bring vision to sight, once
dimmed by fears realities.
The song of the prophet lifts the eyes to view hopes horizon.
The song of the prophet fills the armory with weapons of
warfare to conquer foes both old and new.
The song of the prophet hurls the clouds of doom and defeat
from their throne and fills the skies with eternal sunshine.
The song of the prophet turns the prospectus of life to found
itself in hopes victories.

The song of the prophet gives faith the basis to believe in spite

of adversity.
The song of the prophet raises hope to the level of expectation that will not be denied.
The song of the prophet gladdens the heart and sings of a future to be desired.
The song of the prophet elevates men to the stairways of the Father's plan.
The song of the prophet stirs the spirit within to incredible mountain tops of worship and devotion.

The song of the prophet is the song of the spirit urging, impelling, compelling life's best from men.
The song of the prophet became the cry for freedom when the first slave caught sight of the heart's hope.
The song of the prophet quickens the stumbling feet to run with patience the race set before them.
The song of the prophet showers with radiant light the dark corners of life.
The song of the prophet lights sparks of joy, lifts up the weary and invigorates the despairing.
The song of the prophet must be sung to a weary world groaning in desperation.

So prophets sing your song; its melody waits to restore and renew all of life around you.
Prophet sing your song of deliverance, the drum beat is the very rhythm of life. The whole world waits to respond in joyous rebirth.
SING PROPHET SING, God himself awaits your song to fulfill it.

Rays of Hope

As the sun rises in the east to begin its journey westward, the beginning of days is seen in its rays

the promise of hopes journey onward.
Though the sun always rises
for some no surprises, for their agenda is already set.
In the concrete of despair, their lives are filled with gloom.
No sun on the horizon for darkness fills their sight with doom.

To those prophets of pain,
we say look again
the sun even shines for you.
Its rays promise a new day
filled with a new way of facing and winning your "Waterloo".

Out of the struggle a new man emerges.
Battle scarred but courageous to pursue the pathway forgotten.

No longer in fear cowering,
his knees never bowing
to fates once overpowering,
he stands new begotten
To hopes image renewed for faith to take hold of.
The work now encouraged produces hopes gotten.

The rays of hope sprinkled in life, entice us to achieve destiny's
image.
The person I am evolves to the person I can be.
I now engage life sprinkled with hopes anew.

Follow the Star

Out of the night of faded hope,
Came a new Star of direction
Pointing the way for man to cope.

That night of blessing filled with new songs,
Sung not by men but angel throng

With message so clear "FOLLOW THE STAR"
Men little knew the babe that was
borne held eternity in its hands
Would call men from distant nations and lands
To lay at His feet the riches of kings
There bowed to await his commands.
They only knew to FOLLOW THE STAR.

Wisdom from the east, wisdom of light, wisdom of life,
and wisdom of love followed the star to its resting place.
To find the child of destiny's purpose through its eyes
to see the world of tomorrow.
Not looking to earth for histories past
But looking upward with eyes of hope at last.
WISDOM FOLLOWS THE STAR.

Imagine the wonder of those on that night
Awakened by angels clothed in bright light.
Led to a stable to see what they had seen oft before
A new born child.
Though nothing appeared new except the Baby
Some how they knew that wrapped in the clothes of birth
Was a promise of hope long treasured by earth.
THEY HAD FOLLOWED THE STAR.

The night of long ago still points the way to Eden's
Paradise regained in a garden of Hope, a STAR showed
the way.
While men seek all avenues past and present to
unlock the mysteries of light, life and love.
The path is clear to see for those who FOLLOW THE
STAR in the path from above.

ALL OF HOPE, ALL OF PROMISE, ALL OF TRUE DESTINY
IS GAINED WHEN MEN FOLLOW THE STAR.

Goodness lined her face

Goodness lined the face of loves deepest devotion
Etched deeply the strength of commitment
A face unmatched by Hollywood's greatest photography
Their imitation a poor caricature of the reality of such a
face of goodness.
Such are the images born in the heart of those who call
her - mother.

The eyes that shed precious tears to perfume Heavens
altar of petition Tears that evoked the grace of God for
wayward children
Became the riverbed of mercies received.
Ah, such prayers heard in heaven answered on earth.
Who could connect such different worlds? -- Mother!

The hands untouched by the magic of a manicurist
The fingers plunged into the many labors for little ones
Who at that moment neither noticed nor appreciated
the toils.
That hand ceased not their efforts for children
now grown
They prepared meals for special days - now treasured
Surely such hands could only belong to such a revered
one - Mother.

The body once beautiful now ravaged by the birthing of
her family
Worn by labors so abundant, the mind staggers at the
counting
The shoulders stooped with the years
Lay in a casket of white velvet and cascades of flowers
That she only saw at the funerals of others. Mother.
Yet remembered! Yet treasured! Yet loved! Yet honored!

Never to be forgotten, always to be revered.
Emblem of mercy - banner of love
Monument grace! Mother.

Anthems Raise

Anthems raise in joyous note of victories won.
Their song awakens the heart to a new level of joy and praise.
Hymns of majesty stir up the quiet places of my spirit.

New heights of grace that dispel the darkness of defeat and
failure.
The new song of the inner man usher in the day of fulfilled
faith.
The trophies and plunder of the enemies destroyed, are the
songs played on Miriams tambourine.

The invitation to dance puts a thousand feet to leaping with
unbridled passionate praise.
The declaration of our song is: look at the spoils we have taken.
The ground upon which we dance was once the habitation of
leviathan and dragons.

The territories we have taken are now consecrated by the
anthems we raise.
Purified by praise, the ground has become the planting of the
Lord.
Sing loud with joy, not only for the spoil and plunder, but for
the future harvest now planted by Judah.

Here will the instruments of beauty declare forever the
greatness of our God.
In the perfume of the sacrifice of praise is the pleasant place of
our Father. While some ponder the reasons for the songs and
can only see the superficial.

The anthems raised secure the presence of our great God, where his smoke obscures his Holiest Throne.
Yet He is here on the conquered territory of praise and worship.
Rise up you who sing! Rise up you who play your instruments and blend with the prophecy of His Holiness.

There is much land to be occupied. There are mega battles yet to be fought-so prepare your mouth for battle.
Launch the new songs of your spirit as arrows and fiery darts against all enemies foreign and domestic.
Fill the streets, fill the market places, fill the schools, fill the political arenas with your song and watch the walls crumble and fall.

Raise the anthem in all of its beauty and unlimited power---watch the enemy flee before the Lord of Hosts.

I Must Go On

Who declared it so? Where in the wisdom of life was it engraved, that I must go on?
Wearied by unanswered questions, overwhelmed by the death of dreams, yet living demands I must go on.
In the mortuary of endless days to no purpose, existence continues but life is dead. I must go on.

From the distant past faint memories, before the death and departure of dear ones, remind me I must go on.
Remembering plans of life to conquer, the dreams of cherished future begin to emerge anew. I must go on.
I do not know why I remain when others so much more gifted than I, left life early. Yet I must go on.

The heart still beats, the eyes yet see; the ears are full of hearing. Others beckon me to future that drew them onward. So unfinished dreams demand I must go on.

I SHALL GO ON FOR LIFE IS MORE THAN ME.

CHAPTER 15

PROPHETIC MINI-STUDY: KINGS DON'T BEG

Know you not that to whom you yield yourselves to obey,
his servants you are... —*Romans 6: 16*

ॐ

S ome time ago when asked to pray for a woman's business I was urged by the Spirit to tell her: "Kings don't beg. Kings command." That phrase stuck in my mind as an answer for most of our unanswered prayer.

Namely, we have been beggars at the throne room for God to intervene and miraculously meet needs the father has already declared ours by covenant promise. God is not our problem; our lack of knowledge about our authority has robbed us again and again. "Kings don't beg; Kings command."

All of creation abhors a vacuum. From the beginning, God gave mandate in *Genesis 1: 28*, "Take dominion and in this Adam and Eve failed. Their first and most grievous sin was in failing to take command of their kingdom.[1]

With that vacuum of kingship command, the subtle serpent then got them to eat of the forbidden fruit in rebellion against God. As the result man was banished from his place of dominion.

The garden of provision became a place withdrawn from their access. The world itself became a place of hostility and endless effort. Don't make the sin of the garden all Adam or all Eve. They both had the same authority; neither exercised the dominion they had.

Kings are both born and made. Royalty is first a birthright. It is genetically conferred, the direct result of parentage. God's promise to David was there would be no lapse of his lineage to sit on the throne forever.

Oh weak timorous soul, I ask you in the words of the song of *Toby Keith* "Who's Your Daddy?" You are a joint heir with Christ to the kingdoms of this world. "Kings don't beg; Kings command." David himself was made a King despite his lowly position. His anointing came before he ever met Goliath.

His mighty exploits were the direct result of the anointing that was on him. *1 John 2: 27* declare that you and I have an anointing that abides in us. That anointing will teach us all we need to know about taking dominion.[2]

David ascended the throne of Judah and of Israel after many exploits of courage, energy, vision, determination, and sheer enthusiasm for the battle. It was only after many years of taking command in small things that he proved himself ready to rule a kingdom.

A kingdom is established at various levels of authority. It begins with the kingdom of self. Jesus after his baptism and anointing by the Holy Spirit was led into the wilderness where after 40 days of fasting He was tempted of the devil. The kingdom of self was tested. Did He have command of Himself? Self-discipline will decide your ability to command others. Jesus met all three tests of his inner kingdom, the lust of the flesh, the lust of the eye, and the pride of life.

Each was met on the basis of the Word of God and victoriously commanded. Notice not one time, did Jesus request added power from God to meet his adversary nor did he seek more faith. He used the tools of command that were available not only to Him but to every believer.

Did you notice that, Jesus never asked the Father for power, wisdom nor faith before he healed the sick, cast out demons or preformed miracles? By words of command He executed the purposes of God.

Only at the graveside of Lazarus did he pray and that was only to establish the Father heard him. "I know that you hear me always."[3] *John 11: 41-42* Where comes this confidence and faith! He had been given a Kingdom and he exercised the authority of that Kingdom with out fail.

Are you in command of your kingdom? *Romans 6: 16* says, "Know you not that to whom you yield yourselves to obey, his servants you are..."[4] Picture the absurdity of it; a King bowing to a lesser King. Who's in command of your kingdom? The devil cannot overpower you but you can yield yourself to him. All history, past, present and future is a story of whom is in control?

Don't get religious on me at this point. The Lordship of Jesus in your life is only in the places you have yielded control to Him. If He had total control of you, every appetite, every thought would be perfect and absolutely sinless. I don't know if you've noticed but angel wings haven't sprouted on your back overnight. You are in control of your kingdom; it is only to be an adjunct of His kingdom as you yield authority to Him.

Proper command brings order out of chaos. God is a God of order and system. Satan is the god of chaos. When one commands the body to get in order; sickness flees. When ones life is under command it becomes in order and systematized.

Command begins in the castle and flows outward to the kingdom. Your kingdom is expandable by annexation, by conquest, by purchase and by relationship; Solomon expanded his kingdom by many marriages. David won territory by conquest and thus enlarged the kingdom. Solomon expanded the kingdom by wisdom. Battle may enlarge the kingdom but wisdom builds the temple. Take command of your kingdom.

Chapter Notes:

1. Genesis 1:28.
2. John 2:27.
3. John 11:41-42.
4. Romans 6:16.

CHAPTER 16

PROPHETIC MINI-STUDY: THE STAND OF FAITH

Let the prophet's voice rise in proclamation. Let the prophet write so
that he that runneth may read it and be led. —*Charles Rosson*

☙

There are those who consider the dreamer, the visionary as
a passive mystic and thus discount their place in history
as unimportant. To do so is to misunderstand the place of the
prophets and patriarchs of old. Where is Abraham without the
dream of an enduring city everlasting in the heavens?

Forget the dreams of Moses for freedom for his people from
Egypt; lay aside his dream for a land flowing with milk and
honey. To do so is to be swept into a quagmire of ignorance about
God in history.

The vision is the result of intuited wisdom, born of the Spirits
influence in the heart of a man. Out of the bedrock of divine
knowledge, housed in the reborn human spirit, rises in bits and
pieces of holy wisdom imparted by God.

This is the place of Bethel the house of God, where creativity
explodes with wonderful explosions of power beauty and utility.
The genius of God uses ignorant men to speak profound truths
that amaze men.

God used ignorant fishermen, misfits, impoverished socially,
intellectually all for establishing His kingdom. These twelve
were known worldwide for over two thousand years because

of their relationship with Jesus. Such is the genius of God and the God given dream, it impels men to rise to the highest level possible.

This intuited knowledge from God is an artesian well of pure water that enters untainted by "worldly knowledge" flowing into the ocean of Gods destiny for man. When the dream comes alive it becomes both the motivation and the purpose of my life.

Mine is the purpose driven life for the dream defines my life in clear-cut outlines. Daily renewal of prophetic promise keeps the focus ever before me, as I head for God's plan for me. I am defined by my dream.

Awake!

I have called the nations to awaken to the times. They have seen storms of increasing magnitude, earthquakes, and droughts that left starvation and death in huge numbers and yet they do not discern the times. They do not see the result of sin is always death.

The culmination of time is leading to the final confrontation of righteousness and unrighteousness. What was once whispered in the insinuating tones of scientific knowledge is now openly declared for even little children to see and hear. Because of man's unwillingness to hear the voice of God's prophetic voices, I must now speak in tones that cannot be denied.

I now speak with many voices to alert the Church to the once secret agendas of demonic forces that are covered with the blankets of respectability. I do not speak to bring fear or a spirit of futility; rather I speak to arouse the Church to its glorified position of power.

The Kingdom of God is not lacking in authority and power to defeat every fiery dart of satanic influence. She is well equipped for success in every endeavor. She need only use the tools with which I have entrusted to her.

So awaken mighty one, get out of the defense mode and into a mode of attack. Organize your troops in battle formation with a clear plan of attack as the prophets have heard from God when, where, and how to conquer the enemy. If you do not rise to defeat the foe, then I will raise up a new generation of obedient ones who will!

It is time to think about the future rather than remain in the pains of past defeats. How long will the church remain complaining about how things used to be and wish to return to it? I do not wish for a return to the past! I am the God of now! I am the God of tomorrow! If you are looking at yesterday you are behind times and will never catch up with where I am today and where I plan to be tomorrow.

I have reserved a precious group of those who are laying ambushes for the enemy of tomorrow. They are willing to face the onslaughts of those who walk in an admixture of faith and unbelief. It's better to be criticized as visionary crackpots than to be disobedient to the heavenly vision. Hear o church we do not wish to return to political system of yesterday's comfort. We must establish a new system that is filled with godly men and women who look forward rather than backward. (After all, the past helped to produce the evils of our present.)

We will march into the educational field and take over that monolith of atheism and agnosticism with a new system that begins with the beginning of wisdom: God the true source of all knowledge and wisdom. This is not throwing away the "baby" with the bathwater.

We will retain all that is valuable and worthwhile and at the same time expand into realms that were before now, beyond the scope of the scientific knowledge. For there will be a connecting of the Spirit with the head, the health field, medical, and psychological will be revolutionized by the marriage.

It is time for the light to shine in the dark places. It is time for the salt to savor. It is time for the leaven of divine truth to permeate the social institutions around us. It is time for the Church to stand in the gap and build fences of protection around our cities, states, and nations. Do not implore God to do something while you do nothing! I speak as a trumpet on the walls of Zion. Wake up to the opportunity to deal a mortal blow to the enemy.

Our kingdom is not weak nor is it powerless. "We are more than conquerors through Christ who strengthens us. Rise you who love the battle!

The Stand of Faith

When you are standing on the threshold of a promise, it seems as if the air becomes filled with conflicting images and messages. Suddenly you have to wade through a thousand negative reports to receive one positive message of affirmation. It then becomes a good idea to reject out of hand the negative impulses and to focus on the promise with faith. "It is mine it belongs to me. I will receive nothing less than the fullness of the promise. No compromise and no retreat."

First, I will not give my voice to the messages of doubt and unbelief, not even to deny them; I will ignore them, and refuse them a place in my vocabulary. Because all words are creative, I do not want to give my words of authority even in denial for they create an image that produces fear.

Second, faith is much more than denial it is a positive affirmation of a truth received in the heart and released with the mouth resulting in agreeing action. Denial is often a beak picture of fear lurking in the darkness of the possibility of failure. It is also a revelation of avoidance of the negative result that could possibly happen. It's the old story of whistling in the dark as the pretense of courage, trying to convince both ourselves and others.

This is especially done when walking through a cemetery on a dark night. Some pretend a faith that doesn't exist and cover their unbelief with faith words for the benefit of others.

Faith is not a matter of denial, Faith knows a deeper

reality than that which appears on the surface to be true. This inner knowledge is the result of receiving the word of promise and choosing to believe, "Thus says the LORD". His Word is preeminent over every other word spoken or written. Faith does know not hoping or wishing.

It is building on a solid foundation of trust and obedience to the promises given. My desire is driven by faith and confidence not by inner yearnings. I choose to receive what God has promised. There is no such thing as blind faith.

This misnomer has plagued the Church for centuries, for example, that no rational person could be expected to believe and walk by faith. *Hebrews 11:1* states, "Now faith is the substance of things hoped for the evidence of things not seen." Faith is evidence (indisputable, undeniable proof); faith exists is proof of the unseen.

A *Rhema* word arises in the heart and becomes the basis for an unshakable faith. The faithfulness of God is now the fundamental question; will God keep his word or won't he? I have chosen on the basis of his record and because of my relationship with him to believe that he will!

So when the storms rage and the winds blow I will abort the negative into the grave of forgetfulness. The stance of faith and trust requires me to maintain a regimen of refusal to enter the halls of defeatism. For there lies the bombardment of the conscious mind with the arrows of "what if" "I don't know". I stand on what and whom I do know.

So why wrestle with what I don't know? He does know and I know Him! He will never deny his word or his promises to me. All the promises in the Bible are the will of God. These are his purposes and intentions toward us.

Satan doesn't have the power or the ability to overpower the promises of God. Even when you were lost he could not keep you from getting saved. Once saved, he couldn't keep you from receiving the Holy Spirit.

Nor can he keep you from your destiny of promise! Only

man can negate the promises of God. God won't; you shouldn't. Even if sin has occurred, you and I have a ready remedy: repent, confess and receive instant forgiveness and restoration. Thank God that life in Him opens all the promises to me as available and attainable.

Each one of the promises is filled with *dunamis* -self-energizing power, much like nuclear fission, a chain reaction of unlimited power, Gods power in manifestation. Faith releases God to do what his ability can do! Even faith like a mustard seed in size has enormous ability to grow into a bush that houses many birds.

Your faith will become the resting place for others to nest in. Think of the human seed (sperm) that is invisible to the human eye gestating in the womb for nine months to produce an infant incapable of self-protection and self-preservation.

When finally maturing reaches its designed growth, the result of genes and chromosomes, reaches physical growth after 18 to 20 years of development. And yet we expect dreams and hope to mature instantly. Faith birthed in the heart can leap chasms of impossibilities to bring into the physical world the things birthed in the spirit realm.

I have spoken and I have believed. Now I will act as though my words were true. For in reality my words are declaring my destiny and everlasting purpose.

BIBLIOGRAPHY

Sandra Freeman. *Understanding Prophecy*. Bedford For His Glory Publishing, 2004.

Glenn Foster. *The Purpose and the Use of Prophecy*. Sweet Water Publications.

Dr. Bill Hamon. *The Church Eternal*. Destiny Image Publishers.

Dr. Bill Hamon. *Prophets and Personal Prophecy, Prophets and the Prophet's Movement, Prophets, Pitfalls & Principals*. Christian International

Dr. Bill Hamon. *Apostles Prophets and the Coming Moves of God*. Christian International.

Kenneth E. Hagin. *The Gift of Prophecy, The Ministry Gifts. Rhema Bible Church, Concerning Spiritual Gifts; Plans, Purposes and Pursuits*. Rhema Bible Church.

E. Bernard Jordan. *Giving Birth to Prophecy*. Zoe Ministries.

Author Note: I must mention the hundreds of tapes by Keneth E, Hagin that became my foundational studies in how to be led by the Holy Spirit. Also hundreds of hours of tapes listening to Kenneth Copeland, Jerry Sevelle, Norval Hayes, plus a myriad of other fine ministers of the gospel. I have been an avid reader of books for well over fifty five years. Each or which added to my spiritual education. Even those with which I disagreed. Those tested my knowledge and my commitment to the Word.

ABOUT AUTHOR

Charles Rosson began life in a small house in north eastern Arkansas just outside Datto, Arkansas. He was the seventh child of six living siblings, born on March 21, 1929 and the 3rd son of Thomas Walter and Lessie Rosson.

Later that year, Thomas Walter was already in Flint, Michigan finding employment with Chevrolet Motor Company and didn't see his son Charles, until Lessie and the children could make the three day journey in approximately 3 or 4 months.

It was in Flint, Michigan the family began to establish their roots. Lessie Rosson was already a spirit filled believer, a first generation Pentecostal long before it was accepted as a normal religious practice. A pioneer, she had to develop a thick hide to brush away insults borne of ignorance and prejudice.

At 15 years old, young Charles was forced by his mother to attend a revival meeting. Little did he know his mother Lessie had received assurances from her heavenly Father that if she would get her boys Charles and Wayne to Church that night they would get born-again. Needless to say she did and they did. From Sunday the 12th till Friday the 18th, in time-honored Pentecostal fashion Charles sought to receive the Holy Ghost.

During those five days he brought his Bible to school with him and had begun reading daily. He found the promise of answered prayer in *Luke 11: 13*, "If you being evil, know how to give good gifts unto your children, how much more your heavenly Father shall give the Holy Spirit to them that ask him?"

That settled his resolve in his mind, if God wanted him to be filled with the Holy Spirit and he wanted to receive that gift, they ought to be able to get together. So Friday night after much wrestling with the flesh at a Pentecostal altar (wrestling until the flesh became worn out) he finally acquiesced and received his personal evidence of the Resurrection. The Holy Spirit filled him with the new awareness of things spiritual.

After being filled with the Holy Spirit, Charles was consumed with a passion for knowledge of God. He sat in the "amen corner" with the older men of their church. He read the Bible through in the final 7 or 8 months of the 10th grade. He became aware of the "call to preach" at age 17.

With that call, he also became aware of his need to train himself for that calling. At age 18, he went to their church school Lee College in Cleveland, Tennessee. His formative college years were spent from 1947-1949 at the Lee College; it became his beloved atmosphere of many treasured memories.

In 1949, Charles began ministry as an evangelist then met and married his wife Priscilla Teague. Mr. and Mrs. Charles Rosson entered the pastoral ministry in 1953 and continued from North Carolina, Ohio, Michigan and South Carolina for more than 27 years.

During the latter years of their pastoral ministry the ministry of teaching was developed. Rev. Rosson's introduction to the prophetic ministry did not begin until he was nearly 60 years old. He had little or no exposure to the prophetic ministry until he became acquainted with the ministry of *Kenneth E. Hagin*.

After reading every book he wrote and listening to hundreds of tapes by him and other Word of Faith ministers; he finally learned that he too could hear the voice of God. Since 1994, he has had a singular passion for prophesying to the Body of Jesus Christ.

In 1994, he started a special ministry of teaching young believers, prophets and prophetess' to prophesy. That is still his driving force and mission today.

Other Resources:

Companion Website:
http://www.charlesrosson.com

Prophetic Teaching Website:
You may visit Rev. Charles Rosson at **Prophetic Teaching and Exhortation**: *Know Yourself & Your Future Through Prophecy*
http://livingwaterwords.ning.com/

To Order Books:
So You Want to Prophesy!
Inner Court Publishing
A Division of Butterfly Press
http://www.butterflypress.net

LaVergne, TN USA
05 August 2010
192274LV00002B/62/P